The World Series

THE
World

A History of Baseball's Fall Classic

By Ron Fimrite

Series

Sports Illustrated Director of Development: STANLEY WEIL

The World Series
Project Director: MORIN BISHOP
  Senior Editor: MERRELL NODEN
  Copyreader: LESLIE BORNSTEIN
  Reporters: JIM REYNOLDS, JOHN BOLSTER, RACHAEL NEVINS
  Photography Editors: JOHN S. BLACKMAR, HEATHER BROWN
Designers: STEVEN HOFFMAN, BARBARA CHILENSKAS

THE WORLD SERIES was prepared by
Bishop Books, Inc.
611 Broadway
New York, New York 10012

Cover photograph (Jackie Robinson, Yogi Berra, 1955):
MARK KAUFFMAN

TIME INC. HOME ENTERTAINMENT
Managing Director: DAVID GITOW
Director, Continuities and Single Sales: DAVID ARFINE
Director, Continuities and Retention: MICHAEL BARRETT
Director, New Products: ALICIA LONGOBARDO
Assistant Director, Continuities: JOHN SANDKLEV
Product Managers: CHRISTOPHER BERZOLLA, ROBERT FOX,
MICHAEL HOLAHAN, AMY JACOBSSON, JENNIFER McLYMAN
Manager, Retail and New Markets: TOM MIFSUD
Associate Product Managers: ALISON EHRMANN, DAN MELORE,
PAMELA PAUL, CHARLOTTE SIDDIQUI, ALLISON WEISS, DAWN
WELAND
Assistant Product Managers: ALYSE DABERKO, MEREDITH
SHELLEY, BETTY SU
Editorial Operations Manager: JOHN CALVANO
Fulfillment Director: MICHELLE GUDEMA
Financial Manager: TRICIA GRIFFIN
Assistant Financial Manager: HEATHER LYNDS
Marketing Assistant: LYNDSAY JENKS

CONSUMER MARKETING DIVISION
Production Manager: JOHN E. TIGHE
Book Production Manager: DONNA MIANO-FERRARA
Assistant Book Production Manager: JESSICA McGRATH

Contents

INTRODUCTION / 6

BEGINNINGS / 12

CLASSICS / 20

TEAMS / 100

PLAYERS / 132

FUTURE / 204

APPENDIX / 208

BIBLIOGRAPHY / 217

PHOTOGRAPHY CREDITS / 218

INDEX / 219

Introduction

My own involvement—and I use the word loosely—with the World Series dates to 1941, my first year as a hopelessly committed fan. I was 10 then and struggling against overwhelming odds to become a competent playground infielder. I was handicapped, I knew, by my glasses, which absorbed many more tricky hops than my Ducky Medwick glove, and by a predisposition to panic in crisis situations, such as when a ball was hit directly to me. I did have grit and determination, though, because I'd read that every ballplayer should have these. And hustle was my middle name. But the guys running

my teams usually decided that these attributes were best employed in the no-man's-land of rightfield, where balls were almost never hit. Like many a poor player, I was an ardent fan, a faithful sneaker-in at the Pacific Coast League games of the Oakland Oaks, a regular listener of all baseball broadcasts and an insatiable reader of *The Sporting News*. Since I lived in the San Francisco Bay Area, I saw no major league games—there was no television then—but I followed with ever-mounting anxiety the hitting streak of a local boy, Joe DiMaggio. His team, which never seemed to lose, became my favorite. And through radio and the press I followed the Clipper and the other Bronx Bombers all the way into something new to me called the World Series.

The 1941 Series remains one of the most memorable ever played, not so much for any unusual heroics on the part of the contestants, but for a single botched play. I can't recall whether I actually heard the broadcast of that fourth game—it seems to me I did, riding in the backseat of my great-aunt's Studebaker—but I do know I was immediately aware of what happened. And it changed forever my attitude toward the Yankees. I had learned from painful personal experience that a mistake on the ball field can lead to terrible consequences, but I'd had no idea until then just how terrible they could be. Mickey Owen dropped that third strike, the floodgates opened, and the Series went down the drain. Just like that. The Yankees now seemed to me like bullies bent on taking unfair advantage of some poor soul's mistake. My heart went out to the despised Owen. I felt I knew exactly what he must be going through. And I became a Dodger fan for the next few years, at least until I discovered the Giants.

The next Series that had a personal impact on me came 13 years later, and under much happier circumstances. The 1954 Series opened on September 29, the very day I was released from my 23-month tour of duty in the Army. Drafted immediately after graduation from college, I had been dispatched to fight the Korean War from behind a desk in Stuttgart, Germany. I spent much of my abundantly spare office time following the pennant races in the *Stars and Stripes*, and I'd calculated correctly that I'd be returning to the States just in time for the '54 Series.

I was in a recreation hall at Fort Ord, California, awaiting my freedom when I spotted a television set off in a corner. The opening game of the Series was about to start, so I settled into a lounge chair to watch a rare—for me—game on the tube. And there on the flickering round screen, I saw another Army veteran, Willie Mays, race across the vast acreage of the Polo Grounds to haul in Vic Wertz's stupendous drive to centerfield. What a grand way, I thought, to celebrate my happiest day. I was now a Giant fan, having no idea that in just a few years, I'd actually be writing about them.

In 1962 I was a general assignment reporter for the *San Francisco Chronicle*, assigned to everything from murder trials to bathing-beauty contests. But the city editor, knowing my love for baseball, had pretty much left it up to me that fall to report on the city's reaction to its first major league pennant. I was not in Los Angeles when the Giants beat the Dodgers in the finale of a three-game playoff, but I was in just about every bar and restaurant in downtown San Francisco that day, observing with a keen, if slightly red, reportorial eye the mighty celebration that attended that victory. Delirious fans poured champagne in the streets and danced and sang the night away, effectively shattering the illusion that San Franciscans were too sophisticated to care much about sports. It was, I reported authoritatively, the biggest public bash since VJ Day.

YANKEE JOY IN '62 MEANT DEJECTION FOR THE BAY AREA FAITHFUL.

When the World Series opened the next day at Candlestick Park, I was on the job perusing the stands for "color," which pretty much meant seeking out especially zealous spectators or, since the Giants were then the darlings of San Francisco high society, tracking down tipsy dowagers in baseball regalia. I was at Candlestick also for the fateful seventh game, so exhausted from my pursuit of the unusual and amusing that I simply plopped down on a concrete step in the upper deck to catch the boffo finish. I scarcely needed to capture the fan response to Bobby Richardson's last catch because my own—utter despair—was representative enough.

A few years later I was writing about sports full-time, and a few years after that I was writing about them for *Sports Illustrated*. In my first year on the magazine, I covered the opening weekend of the 1971 World Series between Pittsburgh and Baltimore. It was a tricky business writing about just those first two games,

because I knew that by the time our publication hit the newsstands at least two more games would have been played, and, therefore, any sort of Series overview I might attempt could be made to seem meaningless or even idiotic. A split of those weekend games would leave a writer no opportunity for foolish forecasting, but a sweep by either team would allow for the sort of pontificating I then found irresistible.

Unfortunately the Orioles not only swept the Pirates, they overwhelmed them, winning the Sunday game by the lopsided score of 11–3. And since this was a heavily favored Baltimore team that had crushed Cincinnati in the Series the year before, I decided to throw caution to the wind. "There was no doubt," I wrote, "that the Pirates were on the verge of extinction." They "could only hope that the escape from Baltimore to their carpeted home field would offer them a chance to recoup, or at least to die less ignominiously." As it turned out, I would have a chance to eat those words, for among the more than 300

BOOG POWELL AND THE ORIOLES SEEMED INVINCIBLE IN '71.

pieces of mail I received from irate Pittsburghers after the Pirates won the next three games in a row and took the Series in seven games was a package that contained a copy of my story neatly folded between two slices of whole wheat bread. It left a bitter taste.

Fortunately I would get 18 more chances to redeem myself as a Series prognosticator, and I would wisely avail myself of few of them, preferring, after that disastrous initial effort, to adopt a more reasonable wait-and-see approach. I didn't dare, for example, hazard a guess on the outcome of the 1975 Series, though with a travel day and three more idle days because of rain, I had ample time to develop a host of theories. But this one was so beautifully and thrillingly played, you just wanted to sit back and enjoy the action. I suppose I might have forecast a Boston triumph after Carlton Fisk lofted that majestic home run into the midnight sky of Game 6, but the Reds were simply too good a team to falter, even after so discouraging a loss.

The Series I really looked forward to writing about was the one played in my own Bay Area backyard in 1989. For someone like me, who had grown up with the old Coast League, it was like stepping back in time to days of the cross-bay rival Oaks and Seals. The Giants had won an exciting playoff series from the Cubs and were coming into the Series as the hot team. But the Athletics handled them easily in the first two games in Oakland. Die-hard Giant fans were now hoping for a comeback at Candlestick, and newcomers to that much-maligned ballpark must have thought they were in the wrong place on the afternoon of the third game. The temperature was in the 80's, and there was no suggestion of either fog or gale. The ordinarily turbulent bay off Candlestick Point was as still as glass. This was San Diego's weather, not San Francisco's. It was also, according to local superstition, earthquake weather. And so it was.

Only minutes before the start of the game, old Candlestick shook as if rattled by the hand

10

PITCHER KELLY DOWNS AND HIS NEPHEW EXITED A QUAKING CANDLESTICK.

of Providence. For me, the homeboy, though, this quake seemed not much more severe than any number of others I'd experienced. San Franciscans tend to be a bit blasé about natural disasters, and so when visiting writers sought me out for my expert guess on this quake's magnitude on the Richter scale, I shrugged and said, "Oh, maybe a 5.4. At worst, 5.6." It was a 7.1. A part of the Bay Bridge had fallen, a freeway overpass in Oakland had collapsed, and the Marina district of San Francisco was in flames. The ride home from the ballpark that night through a blacked-out city was one of the saddest I've ever taken. But San Francisco is the most resilient of American cities, and she recovered handsomely, as I knew she would. The Series, which had become an afterthought, was quickly and mercifully concluded by the Athletics when it began again nearly two weeks later.

Ring Lardner called our annual Autumn Madness the World Serious, and I think he was kidding on the square, for, Lord knows, there are many fans who take this sports event very, very seriously. And then there are others like a long-deceased relative of mine who couldn't for the life of her understand why people from all over creation were making such a fuss about the little California Central Valley town where she lived—Ceres. Well, there never has been a World Series in Ceres, but it has been played just about everywhere else over the length and breadth of the United States and now in Canada. And that geographical diversity is part of its considerable charm. I happen to think the World Series represents the best in sports. It has tradition and, as you shall read, a rich history. It does not end in a single day, so the suspense accumulates. And, again as you shall read, the unexpected is so common it must be expected. It is not called the Fall Classic without good reason. It has also become, as I've tried to demonstrate, very much a part of my life.

The trouble is, I still feel sorry for Mickey Owen.

Beginnings

The World Series actually had its roots in the 19th century at a time when professional baseball first began to capture the public's fancy. Until 1869 and the formation of the Cincinnati Red Stockings, the game had been almost the exclusive property of amateur clubs, although it was common enough for some of the more talented members to accept under-the-table remuneration. But when the Cincinnati Base Ball Club formally announced in 1869 that all of its players were salaried, a new era was ushered in, and what had been a genleman's pastime now became the nation's game.

PITTSBURGH SHORTSTOP HONUS WAGNER: ONE OF BASEBALL'S EARLIEST SUPERSTARS

The Cincinnati club, under the leadership of its boosterish president, Aaron B. Champion, had hired a veteran player, William Henry (Harry) Wright, to manage the team—at the then princely annual salary of $1,200—and put baseball in the Queen City on the map. Wright succeeded beyond all expectations. But not without a price.

Wright was born in Sheffield, England, in 1835, but moved with his family to New York City as an infant. His father, Samuel, had been a cricket professional in England, and he soon became the resident professional of the fashionable St. George Cricket Club of Staten Island. Cricket was understandably Harry's first love, too, but in time both he and his younger brother, George, gravitated to the new American game, where their speed and throwing skills were put to best advantage. Baseball in New York had been popularized by the Knickerbocker Club, whose organizer, Alexander Joy Cartwright, had marked off the first diamond in the mid-1840s. Claims made for Abner Doubleday as the game's creator may by now be dismissed as myth, for when he was supposedly chalking foul lines in Cooperstown, New York, in 1839, he was actually 100 miles away attending classes at West Point. No, it was Cartwright and his fellow Knickerbockers who determined that bases should be in the shape of a diamond, that there should be nine players to a side and that three outs per side constituted an inning. The so-called New York Game became baseball as we know it.

Cartwright didn't hang around town long enough to assume much credit for his invention, though. In 1849 he quit his job as a shipping clerk and headed for California in search of gold. Failing to find it, he helped introduce baseball to San Franciscans and then moved farther west to Hawaii, where he died in 1892 as a prosperous businessman.

If Cartwright was the actual Father of Baseball, then Harry Wright was the Father of Professional Baseball. With the blessing of the Cincinnati club he hired ballplayers, including brother George, from all over the country until finally there was only one homegrown team member, first baseman Charlie Gould. Wright whipped his charges into shape by instituting both batting and infield practice. He decided also that his team should have a professional look, so rather than allow his players to take the field in costumes of their own devising, as was the practice then, he dressed them uniformly in jockey-style caps, half-sleeved flannel blouses with soft collars, flannel knickers and bright red woolen stockings. Fans—or cranks, as they were then identified—took to calling them the Red Stockings, a nickname that, with slight alterations, survives today. Wright's fashion statement created a vogue, and even now ballplayers wear virtually the same type of uniform—except that modern players have their trouser legs so unstylishly low, no one can possibly tell what color socks they have on.

Wright's Red Stockings played games from coast to coast in 1869, winning 56 without a loss. More than 7,000 spectators paid to see them beat the New York Mutuals by the surprisingly low score of 4–2 in a midsummer game at the Union Grounds in Brooklyn. And in September they traveled cross-country on the newly linked Union Pacific–Central Pacific railroad line to San Francisco, where they trounced that city's best team, the Eagles, by scores of 35–4 and 58–4.

The Red Stockings' grand tour was an artistic success, and it definitely put Cincinnati on the baseball map, but by the time Champion deducted travel expenses and a $9,500 payroll from the gate receipts, he was left with a net profit of $1.25. Within two years the Cincinnati Base Ball Club had reverted to amateur status, and Harry

THE 1869 RED STOCKINGS: BASEBALL'S FIRST PROFESSIONAL TEAM.

Wright had moved on to Boston, taking the Red Stockings nickname with him.

By the 1870s baseball was recognized as "the National Game," and with a new transcontinental railroad system, the telegraph, typewriter, telephone, adding machine and improved printing equipment, newspapers began covering games so regularly that a new form of journalism evolved, for better or worse, called sportswriting. Among the first and most energetic of these new journalists was Henry Chadwick, born in England in 1824, who wrote baseball for the *New York Clipper* and the *Brooklyn Eagle*. Chadwick was the first to burden the game with columns of statistics, and he joined Wright and Cartwright paternalistically as the Father of the Box Score. Chadwick continued his computations for the *Spalding Official Baseball Guide* until his death in 1908.

The first true baseball league, the National Association of Professional Base Ball Players, was organized on March 17, 1871, but almost from the start it was plagued with financial difficulties and the gambling and game-fixing proclivities of its players. Its deathblow was delivered in February 1876 with the formation of the National League of Professional Base Ball Clubs, a brainchild of William A. Hulbert, president of the Chicago White Stockings. Each team in this new league signed its players to contracts that not only discouraged franchise-jumping but held them in a form of bondage called the reserve system, which stipulated that they could only leave a team's employ by being traded or sold to another.

There were eight teams in the league—representing Chicago, New York, Boston, Philadelphia, Cincinnati, St. Louis, Louisville and Hartford—but the most dominant by far was Hulbert's own White Stockings. Led by pitcher-manager Albert Goodwill Spalding, winner of 47 games himself that year, and first baseman Adrian Constantine (Cap) Anson, who hit .356, the White Stockings won 52 of 66 games to win the National League's first pennant. Spalding would manage just one more year, then move into the team's front office and upon Hulbert's death in 1882, succeed him as club president. As the proprietor of his own sporting goods company, he would also become the

ANSON HIT .356 IN THE FIRST N.L. SEASON.

exclusive manufacturer of major league baseballs and publisher of the game's annual guidebook. Anson would remain with the team until 1897 and become the first player in the history of the game to get 3,000 hits. Appointed manager in 1879, he led the White Stockings to five league championships in the 1880s.

The National League's monopoly on baseball talent was soon threatened, however, by the formation of the rival American Association of Base Ball Clubs in 1882. Because of the reserve system and the ever-present threat of blacklisting, the new league was unable to lure many star players away from the older one, but it did have the advantage of charging only 25 cents admission to its games, half as much as in the National League. It also gave member teams the option of selling liquor in their ballparks and of scheduling games on Sundays where the law permitted. Both booze and Sunday ball were forbidden in the more puritanical National League.

The American Association was also favored with somewhat more creative club owners, one of whom, Chris Von der Ahe of St. Louis, transformed his Sportsman's Park into a family entertainment center with fireworks, food concessions and even women's rest rooms. As the owner of a beer garden himself, the German-born Von der Ahe saw to it that the suds were readily available. He was also something of an eccentric, who enjoyed hauling his gate receipts to the bank in a wheelbarrow. He outfitted his players in expensive silk uniforms and transported them to the ballpark in regal carriages. But for all the showmanship, he fielded excellent teams, his Brown Stockings winning four straight pennants in the 1880s under the management of Charlie Comiskey, who also played first base. He had a major gate attraction in third baseman Arlie Latham, who was known affectionately as The Freshest Man on Earth. Swift and daring, Latham stole 129 bases for the Brown Stockings in 1887 and 109 in '88. He retired as a player in 1899, but as a coach for the New York Giants in 1909 he got into four games and at 49 became the oldest big leaguer ever to steal a base. He was working as a press box attendant for the Giants when he died in 1952 at the age of 92.

A revived Cincinnati "Reds" club won the first American Association pennant, in 1882, and

YOUNG: CLEVELAND'S PITCHING VIRTUOSO.

challenged the White Stockings to a "World's Championship Series." To circumvent a rule then prohibiting play between the two leagues, the Reds released all of their players and then re-signed them to special "World Series" contracts. The two champions played only two games, both at the Bank Street Grounds in Cincinnati. The Reds won the first 4–0 on the shutout pitching of bespectacled Will White, and the White Stockings took the second 2–0 behind Larry Corcoran.

The two league presidents, H.D. (Denny) McKnight of the American and Abraham G. Mills of the National, reached a coexistence agreement in 1883, and both leagues prospered that year, with attendance figures of more than a million for each. Von der Ahe boasted that because of "mein poys," he showed a profit of $70,000. After the 1884 season the championship teams, the New York Metropolitans of the A.A. and the Providence Grays of the N.L., agreed to play in what was then considered to be the first "official" World Series. The Grays had a big edge, though. His name was Charles (Old Hoss) Radbourn, a stocky (5' 9", 168

pounds) 29-year-old righthanded pitcher who accounted for 60 of his team's 84 victories that year, striking out 441 batters in the preposterous total of 678⅔ innings pitched. Old Hoss also completed all 73 of his starts and had an earned run average of 1.38.

In the Series he beat the Mets three straight, but only the first of the three games went the full nine innings. The second game was called because of darkness after seven innings and the third was halted by mutual agreement after six with the Grays leading 11–2. In his 22 innings Radbourn gave up 10 singles and a double, walked none and struck out 17. His earned run average was an even 0.00, the Mets' three runs in the Series scoring on errors. Unfortunately Hoss would never again achieve such impossible heights. He pitched with declining success until 1891 and finished with a career record of 311–194. And his life after baseball would be marred by financial ruin and physical disability. He lost an eye in a hunting accident and was so ashamed of the disfigurement that he retreated to the back room of a billiard parlor he operated in Bloomington, Illinois, and lived

DREYFUSS: AN EARLY SERIES ARCHITECT.

there as a hard-drinking recluse until his death at the age of 42 in 1897.

The National League and the American Association continued postseason play until the A.A. finally collapsed under a mountain of debt in 1891. The National League, expanded by now to 12 teams, again enjoyed a monopoly position. And yet, it missed those "World Championship" Series. A split-season championship playoff was tried in 1892, but the fans found it artificial and dull. Then from 1894 through '97, the first- and second-place teams played annually for the rights to a two-and-a-half-foot-high silver loving cup donated by Pittsburgh Pirate owner William Chase Temple. But the Temple Cup playoffs were considered even more ludicrous than the split-season competition. The press lambasted the gimmick as a "shabby spectacle" bearing no more resemblance to the championship games of the 1880s than "a crab apple does to a pippin." To make matters worse, the league champions lost three of the four Cup matchups to the second-place teams, thereby diminishing the prestige of the regular-season pennant. Cleveland's legendary Cy Young was almost singlehandedly

responsible for one of the upsets, winning three games in six days in the 1895 Cup.

The Gay Nineties were dominated by the rough and tumble Baltimore Orioles managed by Ned Hanlon and featuring such legendary stars as Dan Brouthers, Hughie Jennings, Wee Willie Keeler, Wilbert Robinson and John McGraw. These master practitioners of "inside baseball" won three pennants in succession from 1894 through '96 and established a scientific style of play that would be the norm until Babe Ruth came along a quarter of a century later and introduced the long ball and the big inning to the game.

By 1900 baseball had pretty much assumed the form it would maintain for the better part of a century. The pitching distance from home plate was lengthened from 50 feet to 60'6" in 1893 and the pitcher's "box" replaced by a rubber slab. Pitchers had been allowed to throw overhand since 1884, and the greater distance encouraged the use of deception not just speed. The catcher's mitt was developed by the Giants' Buck Ewing in 1888, and Providence shortstop Art Irwin had devised a padded fielder's glove as early as 1884. The 154-game schedule was adopted in 1898, and it would survive — save for the World War I years — until the leagues expanded in the 1960s.

Nineteenth-century baseball would generate a host of wonderful players in addition to such familiar stars as Young and Pittsburgh's Honus Wagner, both of whom continued to flourish well beyond the turn of the century. Michael Joseph (King) Kelly, who began playing in the 1870s, was perhaps the game's first superstar, a colorful showman who developed the hook and fadeaway slides and inspired the popular Tin Pan Alley tune "Slide, Kelly, Slide!" He was also a drunken hell-raiser and not entirely honest. Once, in the last inning of a game played in gathering darkness, Kelly gave such a convincing impression of catching a long fly ball against the fence that the umpire called the final out. Asked by a teammate how close the ball had come to clearing the fence, Kelly replied with a shrug, "How should I know? It went a mile over my head." Like so many of his roustabout contemporaries, Kelly died young, of pneumonia, at the age of 36.

Ed Delahanty was another of this fast-paced, short-lived breed. He was also the most feared batsman of the 19th century. On July 13, 1896, he hit four homers in one game, a remarkable feat in the Dead Ball era. He batted over .400 three times and twice went 6 for 6 in a game. Once he hit a ball so hard it split in two, and on another occasion he hit a line drive with such force that it broke a third baseman's leg. Delahanty, one of five brothers who played in the big leagues, died mysteriously on July 2, 1903, at the age of 35 from a fall off a bridge over the Niagara River in New York. He had been ejected earlier that night from a Detroit-to-New York train for drunken and rowdy behavior and afterward had grappled with a bridge watchman. He was

then said to have disappeared into the night. It has yet to be determined whether he jumped, fell or was pushed off the bridge. The river current apparently carried him over Niagara Falls, where his mangled body was found on the Canadian side seven days after his disappearance.

Shortly after the turn of the century the National League's hegemony ended abruptly and permanently when Byron Bancroft (Ban) Johnson declared that his new American League (formerly the Western League) was of equal stature and should be recognized as such. More than a hundred National League players, enticed by higher salaries, jumped to the new league, and in the fall of 1902 the N.L. sued for peace. According to a new National Agreement, the two leagues would henceforth operate as separate but equal entities and share common rules. A national commission composed of the two league presidents, Johnson and Harry Pulliam, and Cincinnati owner Garry Herrmann would serve as major league baseball's governing body.

No provisions were made, however, for a postseason series. But at the end of the 1903 season the owners of the two league champions, Barney Dreyfuss of the National League Pirates and Henry J. Killilea of the Boston Pilgrims, agreed to play a best-of-nine-games series. Won by Boston of the upstart American League, this series is generally conceded to be the first modern World Series. But it had no official sanction, and when the Pilgrims challenged the N.L. champion New York Giants to another postseason matchup, Giant manager John McGraw rejected them with the derisive comment, "We are champions of the only real major league."

To forestall future disunity the national commission then took control of the World Series and dictated that the champions must play each year. And beginning in 1905, that, thankfully, is the way it has been.

Classics

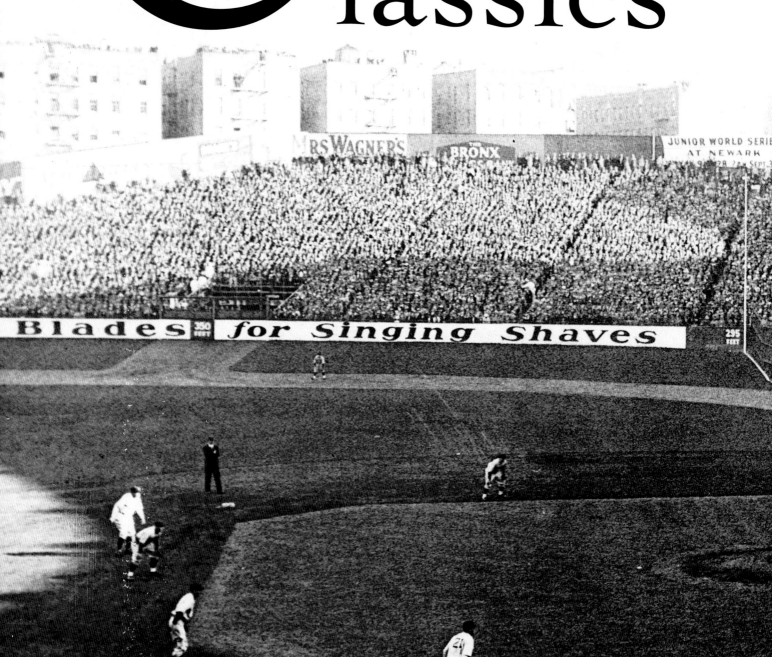

1 9 0 5

New York Giants : 4

Philadelphia A's : 1

JOHN McGRAW, WHO HAD DISMISSED THE 1904 American League champion Boston Pilgrims as "bush leaguers" and refused to play them in a postseason showdown, considered this the first legitimate World Series. And so, grudgingly, did his boss, Giants owner John T. Brush, a feisty man disabled by rheumatism who despised the new league for situating a team, the then Highlanders, in what had been his exclusive New York market. McGraw, though, was so enthused by the prospect of humiliating the upstart Athletics that he outfitted his charges in special World Series uniforms—all black, save for white piping and socks.

The Series would match for the first time two of the game's legends, McGraw and Connie Mack. And had it not been for a ludicrous accident, it would also have paired two pitching immortals, Christy Mathewson and Rube Waddell. It would be difficult to conceive of two more disparate personalities than the Giants' masterful righthander and the Athletics' fireballing lefty. Mathewson, a college graduate, was temperate and cerebral, as clever at games like checkers and poker as he was on the mound. Waddell was a bibulous hell-raiser given to unexplained disappearances and practical jokes. It was the playful side of Waddell that kept him out of the Series and destroyed any chance for a historic pitching duel. Scarcely two weeks before the end of the season,

GAME 1
NEW YORK 3, PHILADELPHIA 0
GAME 2
PHILADELPHIA 3, NEW YORK 0
GAME 3
NEW YORK 9, PHILADELPHIA 0
GAME 4
NEW YORK 1, PHILADELPHIA 0
GAME 5
NEW YORK 2, PHILADELPHIA 0

Waddell, a 27-game winner, tripped over a suitcase on the platform of the Providence railroad station while trying to snatch a straw boater from the head of teammate Andy Coakley. Waddell fell hard on his pitching shoulder and was finished for the year.

That left the stage free for Matty, and he responded with one of the most memorable performances in the history of the soon-to-be Fall Classic. He won the opening game, on October 9, with a four-hit shutout. He won the third game, on October 12, with a four-hit shutout. And he won the fifth and final game on October 14 with a six-hit shutout. No one in Series history has ever approached such sustained perfection. Three shutouts in five days! In his 27 scoreless innings, Mathewson walked only one batter and struck out 18. None of his games lasted longer than an hour and 55 minutes, and he required just 95 minutes to beat Chief Bender in the clincher. Bender himself pitched a shutout in the Athletics' only victory, in Game 2. And the only non-Matty win for the Giants, by Iron Man Joe McGinnity in Game 4, was also, wonder of wonders, a shutout.

With every win a shutout, this Series could hardly be called a bell ringer. And, literally, it was not. To celebrate what was expected to be a torrent of Athletic extra-base hits, the *Philadelphia North American* newspaper erected a huge gong outside its offices west of city hall at 15th and Market streets. The gong was to sound three times for every A's homer, twice for a triple and once for a double. It tolled just five times all week.

MATHEWSON WAS MASTERFUL, SHUTTING OUT THE A'S THREE TIMES IN FIVE DAYS.

1911

Philadelphia A's : 4
New York Giants : 2

IN THIS SECOND MEETING BETWEEN THE PEACE-able Connie Mack and the pugnacious John McGraw, the pacifist won the day, largely through the doings of one John Franklin Baker, known forever after this Series as "Home Run" Baker. But Baker was no Bambino. Although he led the American League in homers for four straight years—1911 through 1914—his highest winning total in this Dead Ball era was 12, in 1913, and he finished his career with a less than Ruthian total of 96 home runs in 13 seasons. No, it was this Series alone that gave him his homeric moniker. Baker's two-run homer in the sixth inning of Game 2 beat the Giants' Rube Marquard 3–1, and his dramatic ninth-inning solo shot off Christy Mathewson the next day tied a game the Athletics eventually won 3–2 in the 11th on a pair of errors. "In those days," the Giants' Fred Snodgrass recalled, hitting two home runs in two days was "an extraordinary performance."

Baker's heroics aside, this was an unusual Series in many respects. It started late, October 14, because the major league season that year ran through Columbus Day, and, after six straight days of rain between Games 3 and 4, it didn't finish until October 26, almost two weeks later. The Giants again wore World Series black, the superstitious McGraw figuring that if this somber attire worked

GAME 1
NEW YORK 2, PHILADELPHIA 1
GAME 2
PHILADELPHIA 3, NEW YORK 1
GAME 3
PHILADELPHIA 3, NEW YORK 2
GAME 4
PHILADELPHIA 4, NEW YORK 2
GAME 5
NEW YORK 4, PHILADELPHIA 3
GAME 6
PHILADELPHIA 13, NEW YORK 2

once, it would surely work again. He was, of course, wrong. But it didn't look that way at the start, when Mathewson, still apparently unbeatable six years after his towering performance in the 1905 Series, defeated Chief Bender in the opener at the Polo Grounds, 2–1. That the game was played there at all was a modern-day miracle since a raging fire had all but destroyed the ballpark in April. Giants owner John T. Brush, surveying the ruins from his wheelchair, ordered that the stadium be rebuilt entirely in concrete. This new Polo Grounds survived for another 52 years, until the wreckers' ball finally did it in.

The opener drew a World Series crowd of 38,281 to the rebuilt park, but the players, believing the seating capacity to be greater than that and worried about their cut of the gate, suspected management of downgrading the attendance. Skullduggery was suspected elsewhere, as well, Giant catcher Chief Meyers accusing Athletic third base coach Harry Davis of stealing his signs. "When he yells, 'It's all right,' it's a fastball," Meyers claimed. Soon Meyers began using no signs at all, but, mysteriously, the Philadelphia batters still seemed to know what pitch was coming, scoring a total of 21 runs against the vaunted Giant pitching staff and winning their second world championship in a row. Baker got nine hits and scored six runs in this six-game Series, and, in the concluding game, just five days short of Halloween, the A's scored a lucky 13 runs, seven of them on seven hits in the seventh. McGraw, believing himself cursed, put those black uniforms back in mothballs.

1912

Boston Red Sox : 4

New York Giants : 3

THE 1912 RED SOX, AS FINE A TEAM AS EVER REP-resented the hub, came to this Series seeking vengeance over John McGraw's famous snub of '04. They got it, rather anticlimactically, on a dropped fly ball and a misplayed foul pop-up. These were the Bosox of Smokey Joe Wood and the peerless outfield of Duffy Lewis, Tris Speaker and Harry Hooper. They won 105 games and lost only 47. Wood was 34–5 with 35 complete games and an earned run average of 1.91, a superlative season. But the Giants' Rube Marquard didn't exactly have a bad one, scoring 19 of his 26 wins in succession.

Odd that with so much excellence on the field, the Series should finish as opéra bouffe. After Wood won the opener, the second game was called because of darkness after 11 innings, with the score tied at six.

Replayed the next day, Marquard outpitched Sox spitballer Bucky O'Brien 2–1. Wood won the third game and rookie Hugh Bedient took the fourth, but the Giants scored five runs in the first inning of the fifth game and held on for a 5–2 win. The sixth game nearly ended before it began in a riot at brand-new Fenway Park as police were called to disperse the Sox's roistering fan club, the Royal Rooters, who, deprived of their usual seats by VIPs, staged a pre-game demonstration on the field, singing, generally off-key, their hymn, "Tessie,

GAME 1
BOSTON 4, NEW YORK 3
GAME 2 (TIE)
BOSTON 6, NEW YORK 6
GAME 2
NEW YORK 2, BOSTON 1
GAME 3
BOSTON 3, NEW YORK 1
GAME 4
BOSTON 2, NEW YORK 1
GAME 5
NEW YORK 5, BOSTON 2
GAME 6
NEW YORK 11, BOSTON 4
GAME 7
BOSTON 3, NEW YORK 2

When I Get You Home Tonight." When the Rooters were finally sent packing, the Giants again had a big first inning, scoring six times en route to an 11–4 win.

Only 17,034 turned up for the deciding game, the no-shows protesting the rude treatment of the Royal Rooters the day before. They missed an astonishing finish. Christy Mathewson and Bedient were tied 1–1 after seven innings. Wood came on in relief for Boston but surrendered the go-ahead run in the 10th. Mathewson needed only three outs for the championship. He induced the first batter, Clyde Engle, to loft an easy fly ball to centerfield, which Fred Snodgrass settled confidently under and then … "Yes," he would say later, "I dropped the damn thing."

Engle ended up at second base. Hooper then lined a vicious drive to centerfield, which Snodgrass, seeking redemption, miraculously flagged down. Mathewson then unaccountably walked the weak-hitting Steve Yerkes, bringing to bat the dangerous Speaker. But Mathewson got him to hit a high pop just outside the first base coaching box. Fred Merkle had an easy play on it, and so did Mathewson, but both stepped aside as the bulky Chief Meyers lumbered after it from behind the plate. The ball dropped, untouched, among the three of them. "It's gonna cost you the ball game," Speaker called to Mathewson. He singled sharply to center, scoring Engle with the tying run. McGraw had Matty walk Lewis to load the bases and set up a force play anywhere. But Larry Gardner hit a long fly to right that scored Yerkes from third with the winning run and the world championship.

WOOD WAS VICTORIOUS IN THREE GAMES, THOUGH A BIT LUCKY IN THE SERIES CLINCHER.

1914

THIS WAS SUPPOSED TO BE A MISMATCH, AND SO IT was, only not the way the experts had it figured. The Athletics, with the "$100,000 Infield" of Stuffy McInnis on first, Eddie Collins on second, Home Run Baker on third and Jack Barry at shortstop and a pitching staff led by future Hall of Famers Eddie Plank and Chief Bender, were supposed to bury the so-called "Miracle Braves." This was the Athletics' fourth pennant in five years, and manager Connie Mack was looking forward to his third world championship. The Braves had earned their nickname by storming from last place in July to the pennant, winning 68 of their last 87 games under the fiery leadership of manager George Stallings. The odds-makers were convinced, however, that this team was fresh out of miracles and established the Athletics as overwhelming favorites. The Braves, after all, wouldn't even have a home field advantage, since they'd abandoned their antiquated South End Grounds in August to become tenants of the Red Sox at Fenway.

GAME 1
BOSTON 7, PHILADELPHIA 1
GAME 2
BOSTON 1, PHILADELPHIA 0
GAME 3
BOSTON 5, PHILADELPHIA 4
GAME 4
BOSTON 3, PHILADELPHIA 1

But not all was well with the imperious Athletics. Both Plank and Bender had signed to play the next season in the renegade Federal League, and owner-manager Mack, strapped as always for cash, was even then contemplating selling off his other stars. He had also made what second-guessers later saw as a grievous error when, with a comfortable lead over the Red Sox in the pennant race, he sent his aces, Plank and Bender, home to Philadelphia a

week before the end of the season to rest their mighty arms for the Series. "They lost their fine edge," said teammate Rube Bressler. "Their control was off."

Both Stallings and Mack managed in street clothes, the only opposing skippers in Series history to appear exclusively in mufti, but their fashion statement was virtually all they shared. Mack was an inordinately calm and quiet sort who eschewed profanity and communicated with his players on the field mainly by waving his game program. Stallings was a noisy, excitable firebrand who, in the words of former player Jimmy Austin, "cussed something awful."

But the blasphemer prevailed, as the Braves' miraculous streak stretched another four games, the first sweep in Series history. Dick Rudolph and Bill James won two games apiece, James allowing no earned runs in 11 innings, Rudolph only one in 18. The losses were evenly distributed among four Philadelphia starters—Plank, Bender, Joe Bush and Bob Shawkey, stars all. Brave catcher Hank Gowdy, a .243 hitter during the season, batted a gaudy .545, his six hits including three doubles, a triple and a home run. He also walked five times.

Mack did indeed break up his team after this disappointment, sending Collins, Barry, Baker, Shawkey and Herb Pennock off to other teams, along with Plank and Bender. It would be another 15 years before the not-yet Grand Old Man would return to the Series. The Braves, hardly miraculous thereafter, wouldn't make it back until 1948.

1919

Cincinnati Reds : 5

Chicago White Sox : 3

*"I knew at the time that some finagling was going on. ...
Rumors were flying all over the place. ... "*
—Edd Roush, Cincinnati outfielder

THE RUMORS, ALAS, WERE TRUE. EIGHT WHITE Sox players, including the team's biggest stars—outfielder Shoeless Joe Jackson, third baseman Buck Weaver and pitcher Eddie Cicotte—had conspired with gamblers to throw the Series, thus entering history as the infamous Black Sox. Also involved were centerfielder Oscar (Happy) Felsch, first baseman Arnold (Chick) Gandil, shortstop Charles (Swede) Risberg, utility infielder Fred McMullin and pitcher Claude (Lefty) Williams. The fixers were to split upwards of $50,000 in cash payments presumably supplied by the Mr. Big of the gambling circuit, Arnold Rothstein. This was big money for players underpaid by parsimonious Sox owner Charles Comiskey. Jackson, one of the greatest hitters in baseball history (a .356 lifetime average), was, for example, earning only $6,000 in 1919.

GAME 1
CINCINNATI 9, CHICAGO 1
GAME 2
CINCINNATI 4, CHICAGO 2
GAME 3
CHICAGO 3, CINCINNATI 0
GAME 4
CINCINNATI 2, CHICAGO 0
GAME 5
CINCINNATI 5, CHICAGO 0
GAME 6
CHICAGO 5, CINCINNATI 4
GAME 7
CHICAGO 4, CINCINNATI 1
GAME 8
CINCINNATI 10, CHICAGO 5

As the betting odds shifted crazily away from the heavily favored Sox, the Reds won four of the first five games, enough ordinarily to win the Series outright. But this year's event was scheduled for nine games to partially compensate the owners for a season shortened to

140 games in the aftermath of World War I. Angered by tardy payoffs, the eight fixers played to win the next two games, and did, before losing the Series-clinching Game 9, 10–5.

The fix rumors took wing, but it was not until nearly a year later that a tearful Cicotte and Jackson confessed to a Cook County grand jury. The eight were indicted, along with several of Rothstein's supposed henchmen, but Rothstein, who reportedly won a cool $270,000 betting against Chicago, was not charged. None of the players was convicted in court, but all eight were banned from the game for life by the first commissioner of baseball, former federal judge Kenesaw Mountain Landis, who was hired to clean up the game.

The fix itself was something of a mix-up. Weaver was in on it from the beginning, but refused to have any part of it, hitting .324 and fielding flawlessly. Landis banned him for not exposing his teammates. Jackson took the tainted money—about $5,000—and then hit .375 with a homer and six RBIs, scarcely the performance of someone trying to lose games. Risberg was more loyal to his patrons. He committed four errors and batted .080. And yet he received not a cent for his dubious achievements. Gandil, the original organizer, walked off with $30,000 and promptly announced his retirement. Cicotte, his able lieutenant, lost two of his three starts and was paid $10,000. But, he told the grand jury, it was not worth the effort: "Now I've lost everything—job, reputation, everything."

1924

THIS WAS THE FIRST SERIES WALTER JOHNSON ever pitched in and the last John McGraw ever managed, but divine intervention or just possibly a diabolical groundskeeper had more to do with the outcome than either of these two immortals. Johnson, then 36 and in his 18th season, lost his two starts, giving up 14 hits while striking out 12 in a 12-inning 4–3 loss in the opener and allowing 13 more hits in a 6–2 fifth game drubbing. But the "Big Train" was there on the mound at the electrifying finish, a winner in relief.

The bizarre events of the seventh game overshadowed some crafty maneuvering by McGraw and his youthful counterpart, Bucky Harris, the 27-year-old player-manager who led the Senators to their first pennant. McGraw had decided to play his rookie first baseman, Bill Terry, against righthanded pitching, moving the veteran George (Highpockets) Kelly to the outfield in games started by Johnson and Fred (Firpo) Marberry. The strategy worked to perfection, Terry hitting .429 in the Series. To defuse him in the deciding game, Harris started Warren (Curly) Ogden, a righthander, but let him pitch to just two batters before bringing in lefthander George Mogridge. This, he reasoned, would get the troublesome Terry out of the game. But McGraw didn't pull the rookie until his third at bat (he was

GAME 1
NEW YORK 4, WASHINGTON 3
GAME 2
WASHINGTON 4, NEW YORK 3
GAME 3
NEW YORK 6, WASHINGTON 4
GAME 4
WASHINGTON 7, NEW YORK 4
GAME 5
NEW YORK 6, WASHINGTON 2
GAME 6
WASHINGTON 2, NEW YORK 1
GAME 7
WASHINGTON 4, NEW YORK 3

0 for 2), pinch-hitting for him with Irish Meusel. Harris then pulled Mogridge and brought in, first Marberry and finally and triumphantly, Johnson.

All the maneuvering in creation, however, could not offset the subsequent vicissitudes of fate. In the bottom of the eighth, with the Giants leading 3–1, the Senators loaded the bases with Harris coming to bat. The Boy Manager hit a ground ball directly at the Giants' 18-year-old rookie third baseman, Freddie Lindstrom, that should have snuffed the rally. But the ball took a crazy hop on the pebbly Griffith Stadium infield and bounced over Lindstrom's head, the freak base hit scoring the tying runs. Enter Johnson in the ninth.

The teams were scoreless until the fickle finger poked the Giants again in the bottom of the 12th. Washington catcher Muddy Ruel, batting with one out and no one on, hit a pop foul behind home plate that looked like an easy out. Giant catcher Hank Gowdy tore off his mask and started after it. He had gone only a few feet before he stepped into the discarded mask and then could not for the life of him dislodge his foot. "That mask just up and bit Gowdy," said an amazed Clark Griffith, the Senators' owner. The ball dropped untouched. Reprieved, Ruel doubled. Then Earl McNeely hit another ground ball directly at Lindstrom. Unbelievably, the ball again hit a pebble or something unworldly and skipped over the stricken rookie's shoulder for the game and Series-winning hit.

"I guess the good Lord didn't want us to win that game," the Giants' Heinie Groh lamented afterward. "That's all there was to it."

33

1 9 2 6

St. Louis Cardinals : 4

New York Yankees : 3

THE CARDINALS PICKED UP A 39-YEAR-OLD PRE-sumably washed-up Grover Cleveland Alexander from the Cubs on June 22 for the waiver price of $4,000. He would give them one of the most unforgettable moments in World Series history. Alexander won nine games in helping the Cards to their first pennant, confirming manager Rogers Hornsby's conviction that old Alex was a bargain at any price. He was also the winning pitcher in Games 2 and 6 of the Series against Miller Huggins's rejuvenated Yankees, who had finished seventh in '25. The seventh and deciding game at Yankee Stadium should have been a day of rest for him, and rumor had it that Alex, who was known to take a drink, had celebrated long and hard the night before. Lord knows, he had earned a night on the town.

GAME 1
NEW YORK 2, ST. LOUIS 1
GAME 2
ST. LOUIS 6, NEW YORK 2
GAME 3
ST. LOUIS 4, NEW YORK 0
GAME 4
NEW YORK 10, ST. LOUIS 5
GAME 5
NEW YORK 3, ST. LOUIS 2
GAME 6
ST. LOUIS 10, NEW YORK 2
GAME 7
ST. LOUIS 3, NEW YORK 2

But in the seventh inning of this final game, with the Cards clinging to a 3–2 lead, the Yankees loaded the bases against knuckleballer Jesse Haines and, with two out, Hornsby looked to the bullpen for help. Tony Lazzeri, a 22-year-old rookie sensation from San Francisco who had driven in 114 runs that year, was at the plate, and Haines, whose worn knuckles were actually bleeding, was obviously finished for the day. Hornsby surprisingly called on Alexander, who had pitched a complete game only 24 hours earlier, to replace him. When Alexander completed his long—and, some say, unsteady—walk to the mound, Hornsby put a hand on his shoulder and confided, "Alex, we're in a tough spot. There's no place to put Lazzeri." Taking in the scene, Alexander replied, "I'll be damned if you're not right. I reckon I better strike him out."

With the count 1 and 1, Lazzeri hit a long drive to left field that, as the crowd groaned, barely curved foul. But there was hope left in the vast stadium. Alexander missed outside with a low curveball: 2 and 2. Alexander came in with another curve. Lazzeri took a violent cut … and, unforgettably, missed. It seemed the air had been let out of the stadium.

Alexander retired the Yankees in order in the eighth and had two outs in the ninth when he walked Babe Ruth, who had already hit four homers in the Series. Then, with slugger Bob Meusel up and Lou Gehrig on deck, Ruth unaccountably tried to steal second. The Cardinals' catcher, Bob O'Farrell, had won the National League's Most Valuable Player award that year not so much for his relatively modest .293 batting average but for his justifiably renowned throwing arm. Ruth was out by a mile.

Alexander and Lazzeri would march in tandem into baseball mythology. Ruth's baserunning gaffe was all but forgotten, quite possibly because he hit 60 homers the next year. But Hornsby, manager of the Cardinals' first world championship, was fired as manager and traded away as player to the Giants a few weeks later. Cardinal owner Sam Breadon explained that he never did like the man.

ALEXANDER WON TWO GAMES AND HAD A MEMORABLE SAVE IN A THIRD.

1 '9 2 9

Philadelphia A's : 4

Chicago Cubs : 1

CONNIE MACK'S ATHLETICS DIDN'T NEED MUCH IN the way of strategy to beat anyone in 1929, for this was one of the game's great teams, one that finished a full 18 games ahead of the supposedly unbeatable New York Yankees in the American League pennant race. This would be the first of three straight Series appearances for the mighty Mackmen. Mack had power with sluggers Jimmie Foxx, Mickey Cochrane and Al Simmons, who had led the league with 157 RBIs, and pitching with Lefty Grove and George Earnshaw, who had led the league with 24 wins, heading a talented staff.

But Mack decided to do a little thinking anyway. He ordered Grove and all the other lefties to the bullpen in deference to Cubs' righthanded hitting stars Rogers Hornsby, Hack Wilson, Kiki Cuyler and Riggs Stephenson, and instead of starting Earnshaw in the opener, he chose the 35-year-old Howard Ehmke, who had appeared in only 11 games all year and had pitched but 54⅔ innings. Ehmke made the old man—Mack was 67 then—look like a wizard, beating the Cubs' Charlie Root 3–1 and establishing a World Series record with 13 strikeouts.

Earnshaw, with relief help from Grove, easily won the second game 9–3, the two aces equaling Ehmke's strikeout total of the day before. But the Cubs won the third game and appeared to have

GAME 1
PHILADELPHIA 3, CHICAGO 1
GAME 2
PHILADELPHIA 9, CHICAGO 3
GAME 3
CHICAGO 3, PHILADELPHIA 1
GAME 4
PHILADELPHIA 10, CHICAGO 8
GAME 5
PHILADELPHIA 3, CHICAGO 2

the Series tied when, entering the Philadelphia half of the seventh inning in the fourth game, they had a seemingly overwhelming 8–0 lead. Then the A's awesome power asserted itself. Simmons led off with a homer, and before the inning had run its mad course, the Mackmen scored 10 times, three runs coming courtesy of a Mule Haas fly ball to center that Wilson misjudged for an inside-the-park home run. Wilson's gaffe overshadowed his Series-leading .471 average and helped produce what remains the biggest inning in World Series history.

The Cubs seemed to have recovered from this disaster, however, and were leading 2–0 in the ninth inning of Game 5 behind the two-hit pitching of Pat Malone when the Athletics exploded again. Malone retired pinch-hitter Walter French leading off, but Max Bishop singled and Haas hit his second Series homer, tying the score. Malone got Cochrane for the second out, but Simmons doubled, and after Foxx was intentionally walked, Bing Miller drove in the Series-winning run with another double.

Third baseman Jimmy Dykes led the winning team with a .421 average. Cochrane hit .400, Miller .368 and Foxx .350 with two homers. Simmons hit two homers, driving in five runs, and Haas led both teams with six RBIs. Grove, pitching strictly in relief, allowed only three hits and struck out 10 in 6⅓ innings. Ehmke, the opening day hero, never won another major league game and retired the following season.

Connie Mack must have known something.

1 9 3 1

St. Louis Cardinals : 4

Philadelphia A's : 3

THIS WAS AS NEAR TO A ONE-MAN SHOW AS ANY World Series has ever been. And that one man, John Leonard Roosevelt (Pepper) Martin, "the Wild Horse of the Osage," was as colorful a showman as the game has ever seen. Pepper was so fond of midget auto racing and tinkering with cars—his real ambition was to win the Indianapolis 500—that he would often show up at the ballpark with his hair, face and hands coated with grease. And by the first few innings of a game his headfirst style of play would leave his uniform smeared with infield dirt and outfield grass. It was he, in fact, who set the sartorial standards of the fabled Gashouse Gang, which he would spearhead in the next few years. Pepper's taste in music ran to such hillbilly tunes as "Willie, My Toes Are Cold" and "They Buried My Sweetie under an Old Pine Tree."

GAME 1
PHILADELPHIA 6, ST. LOUIS 2
GAME 2
ST. LOUIS 2, PHILADELPHIA 0
GAME 3
ST. LOUIS 5, PHILADELPHIA 2
GAME 4
PHILADELPHIA 3, ST. LOUIS 0
GAME 5
ST. LOUIS 5, PHILADELPHIA 1
GAME 6
PHILADELPHIA 8, ST. LOUIS 1
GAME 7
ST. LOUIS 4, PHILADELPHIA 2

But Pepper Martin could play ball. He had been lost for years deep in general manager Branch Rickey's Cardinal farm system and in 1931, at 27, was playing his first full season in the big leagues. At that, he didn't begin to play regularly until June, when Rickey traded Taylor Douthit to the Reds so Pepper could become the centerfielder. Martin responded by hitting .300 as the star-studded Cardinals ran away with the National League race, finishing 13 games ahead

of the Giants and becoming the first team in the league in 18 years to win 100 or more games (101). Leftfielder Chick Hafey won the batting championship by hitting .3489 to the Giants' Bill Terry's .3486 and teammate Sunny Jim Bottomley's .3482, and second baseman Frankie Frisch won the league's Most Valuable Player award.

But the Series was all Pepper Martin. He hit an even .500, his 12 hits including four doubles and a homer. In the pivotal fifth game he drove in four runs in a 5–1 Cardinal victory. He ran wild on the bases all week, stealing five times with his bellyflop slide, and so discombobulated A's catcher Mickey Cochrane that the future Hall of Famer hit a miserable .160. "Pepper is a child of nature," said an admiring Rickey. In the Series he was more like a force of nature. It was appropriate that with the tying runs on base in the seventh game, Cardinal pitcher Wild Bill Hallahan, winner of two games, should induce the Athletics' Max Bishop to end the Series with a fly ball to … Pepper Martin.

After the game Commissioner Landis told Martin, "Young man, I'd rather trade places with you than any other man in the country." Martin replied quickly, "Why, that'll do fine, Judge, if we can trade salaries, too." Martin was earning $4,500 then, Landis $60,000. Actually, Pepper supplemented his meager earnings in the postseason with the $1,500 a week he earned performing on the vaudeville circuit. But he quit his own show with five weeks left to run. Pepper's stage was always the ball diamond.

1932

New York Yankees : 4

Chicago Cubs : 0

WELL, DID HE OR DIDN'T HE? DID BABE RUTH deliberately take two strikes, then point to the centerfield fence at Wrigley Field and hit the next pitch exactly where he pointed, far over that fence? The Babe's "called shot" is now so firmly fixed in baseball legend that the truth may never be known.

The Cubs and Yankees had become bitter rivals even before the first Series game was played on September 28 in New York. Yankee manager Joe McCarthy was spoiling for revenge against his former boss, Cub owner Phil Wrigley, who had fired him after the 1930 season. And the Yankee players were enraged that the Cubs had voted a former Yankee, Mark Koenig, only a half share of their Series cut after he had joined the team for the stretch drive. "Hey, Mark," Ruth had called out to Koenig before Game 1, "Who're these cheapskates you're with?"

That remark and others equally insulting had made the Babe a marked man in Chicago, and so, after the Yankees won the first two games in New York 12–6 and 5–2, he was prepared for a nasty reception at Wrigley Field. As he trotted onto the field for batting practice, nearly 50,000 Cub fans pelted him with insults and citrus fruit. When he came to bat with two men on and no outs in the first inning, the roar from the crowd was deafening, and the Cub players leaned out of their dugout to bellow epithets. Ruth promptly hit a three-run homer.

But the Cubs chipped away at the Yankee lead,

and the score was tied 4–4 in the fifth when Ruth came to bat with the bases empty. Someone had tossed a lemon at him in the on-deck circle, and the abuse from the Cubs' dugout, particularly from pitchers Guy Bush and Burleigh Grimes, had become so virulent that Ruth was fuming when he stepped in against Chicago pitcher Charlie Root.

The first pitch was a called strike. Ruth turned to the enemy dugout and held up one finger. Root's next two pitches were balls. Then Ruth took another called strike. Bush and Grimes scrambled out of the dugout to jeer at him. Ruth held up two fingers and muttered, "It only takes one to hit it." Root, furious with this unseemly display, exchanged words and gestures with the Babe, and Ruth either pointed at the pitcher or to centerfield. The next pitch was a changeup, low and outside. Ruth hit it on a line to the deepest part of the centerfield bleachers, the longest home run that had ever been hit at Wrigley. As he circled the bases, he laughed out loud and clasped his hands over his head like a victorious boxer.

Yes, but did he point to the spot where he hit it? Only one newspaper account the next day said he did, but the legend grew from there, and Ruth never disavowed it. Years later, when then National League president Ford Frick asked him if the shot was called, Ruth replied, "It's in the papers, isn't it?"

Had it not been for the called shot, this would have been Lou Gehrig's Series. He hit .529 with three homers and a double, scored nine runs and batted in eight in the four games. He hit the next pitch after Ruth's legendary clout almost as far out of the park. But nobody remembers that.

A JUBILANT RUTH RECEIVED A HANDSHAKE FROM GEHRIG AFTER HIS LEGENDARY HOME RUN.

1934

St. Louis Cardinals : 4

Detroit Tigers : 3

THESE WERE THE CARDINALS OF THE IRREPRESSIBLE Pepper Martin, of Me and Paul, Ducky Wucky, the Fordham Flash and Leo the Lip. The Gashouse Gang, in other words. The Gashousers remain to this day the game's most colorful team. They were pranksters, roughnecks, comedians and even musicians (they had their own "Mississippi Mudcats" band), but mostly they were tough and gritty ballplayers. Led by player-manager Leo Durocher, they won 20 of their last 25 games to overtake the Giants on the last weekend of the season, but in the Series they would be decided underdogs to the mighty Tigers of Mickey Cochrane, Charlie Gehringer and Hank Greenberg.

Dizzy Dean, who won 30 games that year with seven shutouts, had predicted that he and his rookie brother, Paul, would win anywhere from 38 to 45 games that year. "It ain't braggin' if you can do it," he bragged. It turns out he didn't brag enough, for the Deans actually won 49, Paul—or Daffy, as he was inappropriately dubbed—pitching a no-hitter among his 19 wins. Diz, who had won the game that clinched the pennant only two days earlier, won the Series opener 8–3. He would also win the seventh, while losing the fifth. Brother Paul would win the third and sixth games to keep the Cardinals' Series victory strictly a family affair.

GAME 1
ST. LOUIS 8, DETROIT 3
GAME 2
DETROIT 3, ST. LOUIS 2
GAME 3
ST. LOUIS 4, DETROIT 1
GAME 4
DETROIT 10, ST. LOUIS 4
GAME 5
DETROIT 3, ST. LOUIS 1
GAME 6
ST. LOUIS 4, DETROIT 3
GAME 7
ST. LOUIS 11, DETROIT 0

Diz would create almost as much of a stir on a day he wasn't pitching. He was on first as a pinch runner in the fourth inning of the fourth game when shortstop Billy Rogell, attempting to complete a double play, hit Dean smack in the forehead with his throw, the ball bouncing 30 feet up and a hundred feet away. It is not true, as legend has it, that newspapers the next day reported, "X-Rays of Dean's Head Show Nothing," but there was no damage inside, and Diz recovered in time to pitch an 11–0 shutout in Game 7.

This final game was memorable, however, not so much for Dean's six-hit pitching or the Gashousers' 17-hit attack as for the bizarre events of the sixth inning. Running out a triple, Ducky (his wife called him Ducky Wucky) Medwick barreled into Tiger third baseman Marv (Freck) Owen and sent him sprawling. Since the score was 7–0 at the time, both the Tigers and their fans reacted unfavorably to this display of excessive zeal, unaware perhaps that excessive zeal was a way of life with the Gashousers. The hard slide provoked a brief scuffle, and when Medwick took his position in leftfield in the Tigers' half of the inning, the fans there showered him with fruit and vegetables. When it seemed obvious the disturbance was not about to subside, commissioner Landis ordered Medwick removed from the game so that it might run its course in relative tranquillity. Ducky thus entered baseball history as the only player to be ejected from a World Series game by the commissioner of baseball. Who else but a Gashouser could lay claim to that distinction?

1 9 3 4

St. Louis / Detroit

MARTIN'S RUN GAVE THE CARDS A 2–0 LEAD IN GAME 2, BUT THE TIGERS CAME BACK TO WIN 3–2.

1 9 4 1

New York Yankees : 4

Brooklyn Dodgers : 1

NEVER BEFORE HAD A WORLD SERIES GAME BEEN decided after the last batter was called out. But the fourth game of this one was, and that fantastic finish left the Brooklyn Dodgers, who hadn't been in a Series in 21 years, so shaken that they never recovered. It was the denouement to a remarkable baseball season. Ted Williams had hit .406, the last batter ever to hit higher than .400, and Joltin' Joe DiMaggio had hit in 56 consecutive games, the last batter, in all probability, who will ever do that. But with all the heroics that preceded it, this Series came down to a third strike that wasn't an out.

The fourth game was considered a must-win affair for manager Leo Durocher's beloved Brooklyn Bums. They had split their first two games with the Yankees, a pair of tense one-run affairs, before falling behind two games to one when reliever Hugh Casey allowed the Yankees two runs in the top of the eighth on their way to a 2–1 victory. But Durocher had not lost confidence in his bullpen ace, who had won 14 games and saved seven that season, and he brought him in to quell a Yankee rally in the fourth inning of this critical fourth game. Casey responded by holding the Bronx Bombers in check through the eighth, preserving a 4–3 Brooklyn lead. He retired the first two Yankee batters, Johnny Sturm and Red Rolfe, in the ninth and had

GAME 1
NEW YORK 3, BROOKLYN 2
GAME 2
BROOKLYN 3, NEW YORK 2
GAME 3
NEW YORK 2, BROOKLYN 1
GAME 4
NEW YORK 7, BROOKLYN 4
GAME 5
NEW YORK 3, BROOKLYN 1

46

a 3 and 2 count on the third hitter of the inning, "Old Reliable" Tommy Henrich. Catcher Mickey Owen called for a curve ball on the next pitch. Casey actually had two curveballs, a quick-breaker and a big-breaker, but since the Dodgers had only one curveball sign, Owen was not sure which of the two pitches he would get. He was looking for the quick-breaker, a pitch Henrich later described as, "the craziest curveball I ever saw." Fooled completely, Henrich swung and missed. Umpire Larry Goetz's right arm shot upward. Strike three. Game over. Series tied.

But no. The pitch had also fooled Owen, and the ball caromed off the tip of his mitt and angled off toward the box seats behind home plate at Ebbets Field, with Owen in futile pursuit. A reprieved Henrich, meanwhile, raced safely to first. This was the only opening the Yankees needed. DiMaggio, the next hitter, singled to left, advancing Henrich to second. Casey got two quick strikes on Charlie (King Kong) Keller, moving the Dodgers once more to one pitch from victory. But Keller lined Casey's next delivery off the rightfield wall, scoring both runners. Unhinged now, Casey walked Bill Dickey and then gave up a double to Joe Gordon that brought the score to 7–4 New York. Yankee reliever Johnny Murphy retired the Dodgers in order in the last of the ninth, and the stunned Bums fell 3–1 in the final game on the following day.

"It was as good a curveball as Casey ever threw," a disconsolate Owen said afterward. "I should have had it."

1946

St. Louis Cardinals : 4

Boston Red Sox : 3

TWO OF THE GREATEST HITTERS IN BASEBALL HIS-
tory, Ted Williams and Stan Musial, were abject fail-
ures, and a nifty little Cardinal pitcher, Harry
Brecheen, won three games. But this World Series
was decided by and will long be remembered for a
mad dash on the base paths.

The first post–World War II Series had much to rec-
ommend it. The powerful Red Sox, led by Williams,
Bobby Doerr, Dom DiMaggio, Rudy York and
pitchers Tex Hughson and Boo Ferriss, won 104
games and finished 12 games ahead of the second-
place Tigers in the American League pennant race.
The Cardinals, sparked by Musial and Enos Slaughter, finished in a dead heat with the Dodgers in the
National League and then won two straight from
Brooklyn in a playoff. It was the Cards' fourth pennant in five years. The Series
would also match returning
vets Williams and Musial.
But neither star hit well,
Musial batting a mere .222
and Williams only .200 with
just one RBI.

But the Series itself was a
thriller as the two teams
traded wins through the first
six games. In Game 7 in St.
Louis, the Cards lost a 3–1

GAME 1
BOSTON 3, ST. LOUIS 2
GAME 2
ST. LOUIS 3, BOSTON 0
GAME 3
BOSTON 4, ST. LOUIS 0
GAME 4
ST. LOUIS 12, BOSTON 3
GAME 5
BOSTON 6, ST. LOUIS 3
GAME 6
ST. LOUIS 4, BOSTON 1
GAME 7
ST. LOUIS 4, BOSTON 3

lead in the eighth inning when DiMaggio hit a
two-run double off Brecheen, pitching in relief
after winning the day before. In the Cardinals'
half of the eighth, Slaughter led off with a single off
Sox reliever Bob Klinger, who, because of an illness

48

in his family, was pitching for the first time in 27 days. Slaughter himself had been a doubtful Series starter because of an elbow injury that Cardinal team doctor Robert Hyland feared might involve a blood clot. The team would soon have good reason to applaud his decision to play.

With Slaughter on first, Klinger retired Whitey Kurowski and Del Rice. Then, with two outs, Harry (the Hat) Walker lined a clean hit to left center. Slaughter was running with the pitch. The ball was fielded by outfielder Leon Culbertson, playing centerfield that inning in place of DiMaggio, who had pulled a muscle running out his game-tying double. Shortstop Johnny Pesky had first hurried to second to cover what he thought was Slaughter's attempted steal and then had moved to shallow left center to take the relay throw from Culbertson. The throw from center was not strong, and Pesky, his back to the infield, hesitated before making his own throw. Slaughter, meanwhile, had not stopped running. Angered earlier in the game when third base coach Mike Gonzalez had held him up when he thought he could have scored, he ignored the coach this time and sped for home.

Pesky was caught napping by this daring sprint, and when he finally made his throw home, it was too late. Slaughter's run had won the Series. Walker, who had actually hit nothing more than a routine single, was credited with a double. Brecheen retired the Sox in the top of the ninth to win his third game. And Pesky, the victim of a tiny error in judgment, became another in a long and melancholy line of World Series goats.

1947

New York Yankees : 4

Brooklyn Dodgers : 3

SO NEAR AND YET … IN A SERIES THAT HAD MORE than its share of heartbreaking moments, none can compare with what happened to Yankee pitcher Floyd (Bill) Bevens in the fourth game. Bevens, a righthander, was 31 in 1947. A near-career minor leaguer, he was in only his fourth big league season, and he'd had a mediocre 7–13 year. But he was having the game of his life on the cold afternoon of October 3 in Brooklyn's Ebbets Field. Entering the last of the ninth inning, he was leading the Dodgers 2–1, the lone run against him scoring in the fifth on two walks, a sacrifice and an infield out. Bevens had walked eight batters up to then, but—and this had the capacity crowd of 33,443 on its feet—he was just three outs away from throwing the first no-hitter in World Series history.

Bevens retired catcher Bruce Edwards, leading off, on a fly ball to leftfielder Johnny Lindell, but he walked the next hitter, Carl Furillo. Dodger manager Burt Shotton sent speedy little Al Gionfriddo in to run for Furillo. Bevens then got Spider Jorgensen on a pop-up to first baseman George McQuinn. One out to go! Shotton sent Pete Reiser up to hit for pitcher Hugh Casey, and with the count 2 and 1, Gionfriddo stole second. Yankee manager Bucky Harris now ordered Reiser intentionally passed, Bevens' 10th and last base on balls. Harris had set

GAME 1
NEW YORK 5, BROOKLYN 3
GAME 2
NEW YORK 10, BROOKLYN 3
GAME 3
BROOKLYN 9, NEW YORK 8
GAME 4
BROOKLYN 3, NEW YORK 2
GAME 5
NEW YORK 2, BROOKLYN 1
GAME 6
BROOKLYN 8, NEW YORK 6
GAME 7
NEW YORK 5, BROOKLYN 2

up a possible force play at any base, but he had also committed the sin of putting the potential winning run on base. Shotton sent Eddie Miksis in to run for Reiser, who was nursing an injury.

Shotton then sent up Harry (Cookie) Lavagetto to hit for Eddie Stanky. A popular 10-year veteran, Lavagetto inspired the Brooklyn chant, "Lookie, lookie, lookie, here comes Cookie." He swung at and missed Bevens' first pitch. The next, Bevens' 137th pitch of the game, he hit on a line to right-field, over the head of Tommy Henrich, who lost the ball momentarily against the background of the lower deck of the grandstand, and off the wall, for a double. Gionfriddo and Miksis, running with the pitch, both scored, Miksis with the winning run. No no-hitter. Not even a win.

Gionfriddo also figured in another Yankee heartbreaker in the sixth game. With the Dodgers leading 8–5 in the sixth inning, the Yanks got two runners on with Joe DiMaggio coming to bat. DiMag then hit a mighty drive to the gates of the bullpen in left centerfield, some 415 feet from home plate. But Gionfriddo, who had been shading him to center, somehow managed to cover the ground and, leaning into the bullpen, rob the Yankee Clipper of a three-run homer. DiMaggio watched the famous catch as he approached second base, and in a rare display of emotion, he lowered his head and kicked the infield dirt.

But the Yankees won it all anyway. As usual. And in a final irony, none of this Series' most celebrated figures, Bevens, Lavagetto or Gionfriddo, ever played in another major league game.

GIONFRIDDO COVERED A LOT OF GROUND TO GET TO DiMAGGIO'S PRODIGIOUS DRIVE IN GAME 6.

LAVAGETTO'S LINE SHOT IN GAME 4 NOT ONLY BROKE UP BEVENS' NO-HITTER, BUT IT ALSO DROVE IN THE GAME-WINNING RUNS; AFTERWARDS A DISCONSOLATE BEVENS WALKED OFF THE FIELD WITH AN EQUALLY GLUM DiMAGGIO (FAR RIGHT).

1947

New York / Brooklyn

1 9 5 4

New York Giants : 4

Cleveland Indians : 0

THE NATIONAL LEAGUE HAD LOST SEVEN STRAIGHT
Fall Classics, and the odds were certainly stacked
against the Giants' winning this one. The Indians
in 1954 had set an American League record with
111 wins, finishing eight full games ahead of the
Yankees, who had won 103. Their pitching staff,
anchored by starters Early Wynn (23 wins),
Bob Lemon (23), Mike Garcia (19) and Bob
Feller (13), was considered one of the finest in
baseball history. And they had power with Larry
Doby (the AL home run and RBI champion), Al
Rosen, Bobby Avila and Vic Wertz. The Giants
had Willie Mays back from the Army and a
secret weapon named Dusty Rhodes. In the end,
they were enough.

Take Game 1 in New York: The score was tied
2–2 in the eighth when
Giant starter Sal Maglie
walked Doby leading off
and gave up an infield single to Rosen. The next hitter, Wertz, had hit a triple
and two singles off Maglie
already, so Giant manager
Leo Durocher summoned lefthander Don Liddle
in from the bullpen to face the lefthanded-hitting
slugger. Mays in centerfield played Wertz to
pull, calculating that many power hitters like to
swing at a fresh reliever's first pitch, anticipating
it to be a fastball over the heart of the plate.
Mays was ready. And he was right. Wertz tied into
Liddle's first offering and drove the ball high
and deep to centerfield, where in the cavernous

GAME 1
NEW YORK 5, CLEVELAND 2
GAME 2
NEW YORK 3, CLEVELAND 1
GAME 3
NEW YORK 6, CLEVELAND 2
GAME 4
NEW YORK 7, CLEVELAND 4

Polo Grounds the distances were virtually transcontinental.

Mays was off with the crack of the bat, running full speed with his back to home plate. He caught up with the ball just short of the fence in deepest center, a distance of nearly 460 feet, and pulled it in over his shoulder like a football wide receiver. It was a remarkable catch, perhaps the most famous in all of World Series lore, but he made an even more remarkable throw afterward, holding Doby, who had tagged up and was planning to score from second, to third.

Enter Rhodes: The score was still tied in the 10th when, with one out, Mays walked and stole second. With first base open, Cleveland manager Al Lopez ordered starter Lemon to walk Henry Thompson to set up the double play. The strategy seemed sound because the next hitter, Monte Irvin, had been helpless against Lemon that day, going 0 for 3. But Durocher made a surprising move, pinch-hitting for the still dangerous Irvin with the lefthanded-hitting Rhodes, a part-time player he had previously deplored as "useless" and had tried to trade. Rhodes hit Lemon's first pitch down the line into the Polo Grounds' short porch in right for a game-winning three-run homer. The ball had traveled maybe 200 feet fewer than Wertz's famous out. Such was life in the Polo Grounds.

Dusty also homered in the second game, and he drove in two runs with a pinch single in Game 3. He was 4 for 6 for the Series with seven RBIs. The Indians never had a chance.

1955

Brooklyn Dodgers : 4

New York Yankees : 3

THE DODGERS, LOSERS IN SEVEN PREVIOUS WORLD Series, would finally win one, and Casey Stengel, the winning manager in five straight Series, from 1949 through '53, would finally lose one. But it took some hefty hitting by Duke Snider, who had four homers and drove in seven runs; some gritty pitching by Dodger lefty Johnny Podres, who won Game 3 on his 23rd birthday and Game 7 four days later; and a sensational defensive play by Sandy Amoros to pull it out for the long-frustrated Bums after they had lost the first two games. And it helped that Mickey Mantle, nursing an injured leg, appeared in only three Series games and batted just .200 with only one RBI. It was, nevertheless, a sluggers' Series, the two teams combining for a record 17 home runs, including five apiece in the first and fifth games.

Young Podres was, however, immune from the fence-busting. He held the Yanks to three runs (two earned) on his birthday and shut them out 2–0 in the deciding game. Gil Hodges had driven in both Dodger runs in the finale, on a single in the fourth inning following Roy Campanella's double and on a bases-loaded sacrifice fly in the sixth. But the Yankees appeared to be mounting a rally in the home half of the the sixth when Billy Martin walked leading off and Gil McDougald beat out a bunt, bringing the dangerous Yogi

GAME 1
NEW YORK 6, BROOKLYN 5
GAME 2
NEW YORK 4, BROOKLYN 2
GAME 3
BROOKLYN 8, NEW YORK 3
GAME 4
BROOKLYN 8, NEW YORK 5
GAME 5
BROOKLYN 5, NEW YORK 3
GAME 6
NEW YORK 5, BROOKLYN 1
GAME 7
BROOKLYN 2, NEW YORK 0

56

Berra to the plate with nobody out and the tying runs on base. Berra already had 10 hits, more than any other player in the Series.

Amoros, a lefthanded Cuban playing only his second big league season, had entered the game that inning as a defensive replacement in leftfield. He was shading the hard-hitting Berra to center when Yogi sliced a line drive just inside the foul line in left. Somehow, Amoros got there, and stretching his 5' 7½" frame to the fullest, reached out and made a one-handed catch. If he had been righthanded, the ball would probably have dropped for a double that could have tied the score and put Berra on second with no outs. But Amoros not only made the catch, one of the most famous in Series history, he also hit cutoff man Pee Wee Reese with his return throw, and Reese's relay to Hodges doubled McDougald off first base. It was the play of the Series, and Podres breezed the rest of the way to the shutout victory.

The Dodgers thus became the first team to win a seven-game Series after losing the first two games. Their other wins were credited to rookie Roger Craig, who started Game 5, and to Clem Labine, who won a wild 8–5 fourth game in relief. Whitey Ford, always at his best in the Series, won two games for the Yankees, inluding a complete-game masterpiece in Game 6. Another Yankee lefty, Tommy Byrne, went all the way for the victory in Game 2. But this Series belonged to Podres and to little Amoros, who would, in a career that lasted four more years, have just this one moment in the sun.

1955

Brooklyn / New York

ROBINSON (LEFT) FAILED TO DRIVE IN FURILLO IN GAME 1; SNIDER (ABOVE LEFT) WAS ALL SMILES AFTER HITTING HIS SECOND HOMER IN GAME 5; EVEN STENGEL'S JAWING (ABOVE) COULDN'T PREVENT A BROOKLYN VICTORY AND THE RESULTING CELEBRATION (BELOW).

1 9 5 6

New York Yankees : 4

Brooklyn Dodgers : 3

THE YANKEES BECAME A MIRROR IMAGE OF THE Dodgers of the year before, losing the first two games and then rallying to win. And one of those wins was for the ages.

Don Larsen, a 6' 4" righthander from Michigan City, Indiana, had not survived two innings in a 13–8 Dodger win in Game 2, but manager Casey Stengel called on him as his starter in Game 5, with the Series tied at two games apiece. Pitching without a windup, Larsen offered a hint of what was to come by striking out the first two hitters, Junior Gilliam and Pee Wee Reese. He was flawless thereafter, pitching not only the first no-hitter in World Series history but the first perfect game. In fact, his was the first perfect game in the big leagues since Charlie Robertson of the White Sox blanked Detroit in 1922. With only one batter, Reese, in the first, did the count reach three balls, and there were only three occasions when a fair ball might have become a hit. In the second inning Andy Carey at third got a glove on Jackie Robinson's line drive and deflected the ball to short-

GAME 1
BROOKLYN 6, NEW YORK 3
GAME 2
BROOKLYN 13, NEW YORK 8
GAME 3
NEW YORK 5, BROOKLYN 3
GAME 4
NEW YORK 6, BROOKLYN 2
GAME 5
NEW YORK 2, BROOKLYN 0
GAME 6
BROOKLYN 1, NEW YORK 0
GAME 7
NEW YORK 9, BROOKLYN 0

stop Gil McDougald, who was able to throw out the aging Dodger star at first. In the fifth Mickey Mantle made a shoetop catch of Gil Hodges' long drive. Finally, in the eighth, Hodges hit a hard shot down the third base line that

60

Carey snared. Both Duke Snider and Sandy Amoros hit balls into the rightfield seats that were barely foul. Larsen was otherwise untouchable. He threw only 97 pitches and struck out seven, five in the first four innings.

In the ninth, with the huge crowd of 64,519 howling exhortations, Larsen retired Carl Furillo on a fly ball to Hank Bauer in right and Roy Campanella on a ground ball to Billy Martin at second. That brought up lefthanded-hitting Dale Mitchell as a pinch hitter for Dodger starter Sal Maglie, who had himself given up only five hits and two runs, one on a Mantle homer. Larsen's first pitch to Mitchell was high and out of the strike zone. His next was a called strike. Mitchell swung and missed for strike two, then fouled off another pitch. Larsen zoomed a fastball past him for a called third strike. His catcher, Yogi Berra, raced out from behind the plate and leaped into Larsen's arms, creating a memorable World Series tableau.

The Dodgers recovered from this stunning setback to win Game 6, 1–0, behind Clem Labine, but then the Yankees destroyed them in a third straight shutout game, 9–0, with Johnny Kucks pitching a three-hitter. It was the Yankees' 17th World Series championship, the sixth under Stengel. It was also the last subway Series, spelling the end of a golden decade in New York baseball, during which teams from the city appeared in seven of the 10 World Series since 1947. The Yankees would continue to uphold the tradition, but the Dodgers and Giants would fall on harder times and in 1958 flee Gotham for California.

61

McDougald (above) managed only three hits at the plate, but made a fielding gem to preserve Larsen's perfect game; a wistful Stengel contemplated his sixth world title.

1 9 5 6

New York / Brooklyn

1 9 6 0

Pittsburgh Pirates : 4

New York Yankees : 3

MAZEROSKI'S SOLO BLAST ENDED PERHAPS THE WILDEST GAME IN SERIES HISTORY.

WHITEY FORD PITCHED TWO SHUTOUTS. THE YAN-kees won games by scores of 16–3, 10–0 and 12–0; they had 91 hits, 27 of them for extra bases; they hit 10 homers, batted .338 as a team and scored a Series record 55 runs. Their second base-man, Bobby Richardson, set records for most RBIs in a game—six, in Game 3—and in a Series, with 12. The Pirates batted .256, had only four homers and scored 27 runs, not quite half as many as their opponents. So guess who won? Wrong. For all the Yankee bombardment, this Series would end with a single swing of the bat. It would also be the last time Casey Stengel would manage the Yankees.

Old Case was lambasted afterward for holding Ford back until Game 3 at Yankee Stadium. If the veteran lefty had started the first game, so the second-guessing went, he would have been available for a third start in Game 7, thus possibly averting disas-ter. But Casey stuck to his guns: Ford had won only 12 games that season, had had a shoulder problem and just wasn't up to pitching in three games.

It's also questionable how much of a difference even Ford could have made in a game as crazy as the sev-enth. Vernon Law of the Pirates and Bob Turley for New York were the starters, but both were long gone by the socko finish. The Pirates, in fact, scored twice in the first on Rocky Nelson's homer

GAME 1
PITTSBURGH 6, NEW YORK 4
GAME 2
NEW YORK 16, PITTSBURGH 3
GAME 3
NEW YORK 10, PITTSBURGH 0
GAME 4
PITTSBURGH 3, NEW YORK 2
GAME 5
PITTSBURGH 5, NEW YORK 2
GAME 6
NEW YORK 12, PITTSBURGH 0
GAME 7
PITTSBURGH 10, NEW YORK 9

THE CELEBRATION WAS WELL UNDERWAY BY THE TIME MAZEROSKI REACHED THIRD. BUT A
QUESTION REMAINS: COULD FORD (RIGHT) HAVE STOPPED THE PIRATES IN GAME 7?

and twice more in the second on Bill Virdon's two-run single. The Yankees went ahead 5–4 in the sixth on a three-run homer by Yogi Berra, and a tired Elroy Face (this was his fourth game in relief) gave up two more Yankee runs in the eighth for 7–4. Then, in the home half of the eighth, Pirate pinch-hitter Gino Cimoli singled off Bobby Shantz and Virdon followed with a ground ball to short that had the makings of a cinch double play. Instead, the ball hit something on the notoriously hard Forbes Field infield, took a bad hop and struck Tony Kubek in the windpipe. Everybody safe. And Kubek, who couldn't speak for several minutes, was forced to leave the game. Singles by Dick Groat and Roberto Clemente brought the Pirates to within a run, and then reserve catcher Hal Smith sent the home crowd into a frenzy with a three-run homer that pushed them ahead 9–7. But—will the action never cease?—the Yankees tied the score in their half of the ninth on four singles.

Ralph Terry was on the mound for the Yankees in the bottom of the ninth to pitch to Bill Mazeroski, leading off. Terry's first pitch was a ball. Mazeroski hit the next one, a high slider, over the ivy-covered wall in leftfield and into the trees beyond as Berra, the leftfielder, watched forlornly. The exuberant Maz skipped around the base paths and leaped into the arms of his joyous teammates at home plate. It was another World Series moment.

Five days later Yankee owners Del Webb and Dan Topping fired the 70-year-old Stengel. "Most people are dead at my age," Casey reasoned, "at the present time, at least."

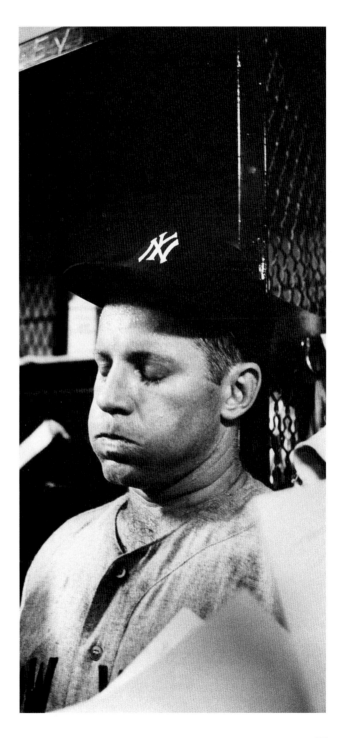

1962

THIS FIRST TRANSCONTINENTAL SERIES HAD A LITTLE bit of everything, including lots of weather. A one-day rain delay in New York was nothing out of the ordinary, but the biblical downpour that drenched San Francisco for three days in a normally balmy season certainly was. With all the unexpected precipitation, this Series stretched to 13 days, the longest since 1911. And the last of those days was a heart-wrenching one for San Francisco fans, who had already suffered through a nail-biting season. The Giants, in fact, didn't win the pennant until the day before the Series was to begin, edging the Dodgers in L.A. with a four-run, ninth inning rally in the final of a three-game playoff.

The Yankees beat this emotionally exhausted team 6–2 in the opener at Candlestick Park behind Whitey Ford, whose streak of 33⅔ scoreless World Series innings was, however, terminated in the second inning. The two teams traded wins the rest of the way—when they could play—setting up the seventh-game dramatics at soggy Candlestick. The Yankees scored their only run in the fifth inning when Bill Skowron raced home on a bases-loaded, no-out grounder hit by Tony Kubek. Jack Sanford, a shutout winner in Game 2, held them in check the rest of the way, scattering seven hits.

In the last of the ninth, Ralph Terry, Bill Mazeroski's victim in 1960, had a two-hitter and the thin 1–0 lead.

GAME 1
NEW YORK 6, SAN FRANCISCO 2
GAME 2
SAN FRANCISCO 2, NEW YORK 0
GAME 3
NEW YORK 3, SAN FRANCISCO 2
GAME 4
SAN FRANCISCO 7, NEW YORK 3
GAME 5
NEW YORK 5, SAN FRANCISCO 3
GAME 6
SAN FRANCISCO 5, NEW YORK 2
GAME 7
NEW YORK 1, SAN FRANCISCO 0

The first batter, pinch-hitter Matty Alou, reached base on a bunt single. His brother Felipe and Chuck Hiller (who had hit a grand slam homer in Game 4) tried to sacrifice him to second, but both struck out. Then Willie Mays lined a double to right, keeping San Francisco's hopes alive. Roger Maris, plodding over rain-sodden terrain, fielded the ball so cleanly and made such a strong throw that Alou was forced to hold at third. Matty said later he might have scored even with Maris's accurate throw had he not been "slipping all the way" on the base paths. But now Mays was on second and Alou on third with the mighty Willie McCovey coming to bat.

Ralph Houk, who had replaced Casey Stengel as manager that year, ambled out to the mound to discuss the perilous situation with his pitcher. With first base open, Houk could have elected to walk the lefthanded McCovey so that Terry, a righthander, might pitch to the righthanded Orlando Cepeda, a .158 hitter in this Series. Or he could bring in a lefthander to pitch to McCovey. But Terry, perhaps seeking redemption for Mazeroski, pleaded to stay in and face McCovey. Houk acquiesced. McCovey hit Terry's first pitch deep to rightfield, foul by only a few feet. He took the next pitch for a ball. Then Terry threw him a soft curve. McCovey hit a vicious line drive toward right center. "My heart was in my throat," said Terry, fearing he'd lost another one down the wire. But Bobby Richardson, perfectly positioned, gathered the ball in at eye level for the final and, for San Franciscans, unforgettable last out.

The Yankees would not win another Series for 15 years.

THE MIGHTY MAYS (LEFT) WAS HELD IN CHECK, DRIVING IN
JUST ONE RUN; TERRY, A GOAT IN '60, WAS REDEEMED, PITCHING A PAIR
OF COMPLETE-GAME WINS, INCLUDING A TENSE GAME 7.

1 9 6 9

New York Mets : 4

Baltimore Orioles : 1

STAND ASIDE MIRACLE BRAVES OF 1914 FOR THE Miracle Mets of 1969. In seven previous seasons, this beleaguered expansion team had never finished higher than ninth and had become something of a national measuring rod for incompetence and lunacy. But the joke was over in '69. Led by a demanding manager, Gil Hodges, and ignited by youthful pitchers Jerry Koosman and Tom Seaver, the Mets played .760 (38–12) baseball in their last 50 games to overtake the Chicago Cubs of Billy Williams and Ron Santo and win the National League East by eight games in this first year of divisional play. They then swept the Atlanta Braves three straight in the first of the league play-offs. Still, they were considered in well over their young heads against an Oriole team that had

GAME 1
BALTIMORE 4, NEW YORK 1
GAME 2
NEW YORK 2, BALTIMORE 1
GAME 3
NEW YORK 5, BALTIMORE 1
GAME 4
NEW YORK 2, BALTIMORE 1
GAME 5
NEW YORK 5, BALTIMORE 3

won 109 games and was deemed by many the best in baseball since the 1961 Yankees.

Indeed, the Orioles won the opener 4–1, Mike Cuellar besting Seaver. But Koosman won the second game 2–1, and after centerfielder Tommie Agee personally took charge of the third game, the Mets were title-bound. Agee started his game by hitting a leadoff homer off Jim Palmer, the fifth time that season he had led off a game with a home run. Then in the fourth inning, with two runners on base, he raced to the 396-foot sign in left centerfield at Shea Stadium to make a thrilling backhanded catch of a poten-

tial triple by Elrod Hendricks. Finally in the seventh, with two outs and the bases loaded, Agee made a diving catch of Paul Blair's liner to right center. All alone, Agee made a difference of six runs in this one game.

He wasn't the only New York defensive star, though. In the ninth inning of Game 4, with the Mets clinging to a 1–0 lead, Frank Robinson and Boog Powell both singled off Seaver. Brooks Robinson then hit a shot to right that could have given Baltimore the lead, but Ron Swoboda, scarcely renowned for his fielding prowess, made a diving, sliding catch. Frank Robinson scored tagging up, but the catch had saved a run. And in the 10th, the Mets scored the winning run on a controversial play when Oriole pitcher Pete Richert's throw to first hit the Mets' J.C. Martin and pinch-runner Rod Gaspar streaked home from second. Home runs by Series MVP Donn Clendenon, his third of the Series, and by light-hitting Al Weis, his third of the *season*, overcame an early Oriole lead in Game 5 and more Baltimore fielding boo-boos in the eighth inning, by Powell and pitcher Eddie Watt, along with doubles by Cleon Jones and Swoboda gave the Mets their miracle championship.

In the end, though, it was a triumph of pitching. The Orioles batted only .146 as a team. Brooks Robinson was 1 for 19, Frank Robinson hit a mere .188, and the powerful Powell had no extra-base hits.

Maybe all this shouldn't have come as a surprise. This, after all, was the year men walked on the moon.

1 9 6 9

New York / Baltimore

AGEE'S HEROICS, INCLUDING A LEADOFF HOMER (LEFT), ENSURED A MET VICTORY IN GAME 3; AFTER
JONES MADE THE FINAL SERIES OUT (ABOVE), SHEA STADIUM ERUPTED IN CELEBRATION.

1972

Oakland A's : 4

Cincinnati Reds : 3

THIS SERIES GAVE US THE BIRTH OF ONE DYNASTY and the incubation of another, but nobody knew that at the time. The Athletics had only been in Oakland since 1968, and mainly because their owner, Charles O. Finley, was such an incurable cornball and irritating presence in the community, nobody there much cared about them. The attendance that year of 921,323 is about a third of what the Oakland champions of the late 1980s and early '90s would draw under different ownership. And in Cincinnati, manager Sparky Anderson was just starting to assemble what in a few short years would become the invincible Big Red Machine.

"The Swingin' A's," as Finley preferred to call them, would have their turn first. They would be handicapped in the Series, though, by the loss of slugger Reggie Jackson, who suffered a hamstring pull during the five-game playoff win over Detroit and had yet to prove his propensity for October heroics. No matter. As this resourceful team would prove time and again over the next three years, there would always be someone around to take up the slack. This year it was Gene Tenace.

Tenace hit only .225 with five home runs during the regular season while doing a little catching, playing a little first base. In the Series opener

he hit homers his first two times at bat, the first time that had ever been accomplished in a World Series. In Game 2, Tenace stepped aside for the moment to allow teammate Joe Rudi to shine. With the A's leading 2–0, Tony Perez led off the ninth inning with a single. The next hitter, Dennis Menke, lofted a towering drive to leftfield that appeared to be the game-tying home run off reliever Rollie Fingers. But Rudi, splaying himself face-first against the green board fence at Riverfront Stadium, reached up and caught the ball backhanded at the very rim. "I didn't think I had a chance," Rudi said afterward. "I thought it was gone." Instead, it became one of the great catches in Series history.

This was another pitchers' Series, and not incidentally because the games in Oakland started at 5:15 p.m., for the benefit of eastern television audiences, a time when the western sun shines brightly down on the batter's box. It was also a relief pitchers' Series, the first of its kind. Not one starter on either team pitched a complete game, Fingers for Oakland relieving in six games, Clay Carroll for Cincinnati in five. Oakland's Catfish Hunter came the closest to finishing, going 8⅔ innings in a 3–2 Game 1 victory. The two teams hit an identical .209 and six of the seven Series contests were decided by a single run. Tenace, who had four homers and nine RBIs, was, ultimately, the edge.

As a franchise the Athletics hadn't been in a World Series since 1931. In the early 1970s, they would become a fixture there.

RUDI WENT TO THE WALL TO HAUL IN MENKE'S TOWERING BLAST IN GAME 2.

TENACE WAS THE HERO AT THE PLATE, WHILE FINGERS (RIGHT) SHONE ON THE MOUND.

1975

Cincinnati Reds : 4

Boston Red Sox : 3

THE BEST OF THEM ALL? QUITE POSSIBLY. IT'S certain this one had all the attributes of a classic. Five of the seven games were decided by one run. Six of the seven were won by the team that came from behind. Two were decided in the ninth inning and two in extra innings. And the sixth game must rank among the most exciting games ever played in a World Series.

The Red Sox, behind the five-hit pitching of the veteran Cuban trickster Luis Tiant, won the opener at Fenway Park 6–0. The Reds came back the next day in a game delayed by rain for 27 minutes to score two runs in the ninth and win 3–2. The third, in Cincinnati, was a thriller blemished by a controversial call—or noncall—by plate umpire Larry Barnett. With the score tied 5–5 in the bottom of the 10th, the Reds' Cesar Geronimo singled leading off. Ed Armbrister, pinch-hitting for reliever Rawley Eastwick, dropped a bunt directly in front of the plate. But instead of running, Armbrister stood motionless for a second, and Red Sox catcher Carlton Fisk, going for the ball, collided with him. Fisk shoved the runner aside and then threw wildly into centerfield trying to catch Geronimo at second. Geronimo advanced to third on the error and Armbrister to second. Fisk and the Red Sox protested angrily that Armbrister had interfered with his

GAME 1
BOSTON 6, CINCINNATI 0
GAME 2
CINCINNATI 3, BOSTON 2
GAME 3
CINCINNATI 6, BOSTON 5
GAME 4
BOSTON 5, CINCINNATI 4
GAME 5
CINCINNATI 6, BOSTON 2
GAME 6
BOSTON 7, CINCINNATI 6
GAME 7
CINCINNATI 4, BOSTON 3

attempt to field the ball, but Barnett held that the collision was accidental and, therefore, that no interference was involved. Much rule book brandishing ensued but to no avail. Two batters later, Joe Morgan singled home the winning run.

The teams traded wins in Games 4 and 5, and then Game 6 ran its tortuous course. The Reds had a 6–3 lead with two outs in the eighth when pinch-hitter Bernie Carbo tied the game with a three-run home run. In the Boston half of the ninth, Denny Doyle's foolish attempt to score from third on a short fly to left killed a Sox rally when George Foster easily threw him out at the plate. In the 11th, Dwight Evans squelched a Reds' rally by reaching into the rightfield seats to take a home run away from Morgan. His return throw doubled Ken Griffey off first. Two outs instead of two runs.

Then, at 34 minutes past midnight, Fisk hit a low sinker thrown by Pat Darcy, the Reds' eighth pitcher of the game, on a high arc down the leftfield line. Fisk took a few dancing steps toward first, urging the ball fair with body English and semaphoring, and then soared for joy as it struck high on the foul pole screen for the homer that won a game that even Pete Rose of the losing team described as the best he'd ever been in. The Fenway Park organist played Handel's *Hallelujah Chorus* over the public address system as long-frustrated Boston fans wept in happiness. But the celebration was short-lived, as Morgan's ninth-inning bloop single off rookie Jim Burton scored Rose the next night with the Series winner. But it was a doozy while it lasted.

FISK'S HISTORIC HOMER ENDED AN UNFORGETTABLE GAME 6.

ROSE WAS TAGGED OUT BY FISK ON THIS PLAY IN GAME 5, BUT LED ALL SERIES BATTERS WITH
10 HITS; AFTER THE FINAL OUT, JOHNNY BENCH HOISTED RELIEVER WILL McENANEY (RIGHT, ABOVE)
AND LATER, IN THE LOCKER ROOM, A CELEBRATORY BOTTLE OF CHAMPAGNE.

1 9 7 9

Pittsburgh Pirates : 4

Baltimore Orioles : 3

REMEMBER FAMILY VALUES? WELL, THIS SERIES was awash in them. The Pittsburgh Pirates called themselves a "fam-a-lee." Their theme song, played interminably at Three Rivers Stadium, was Sister Sledge's "We Are Family." Their paterfamilias was the 38-year-old Willie (Pops) Stargell, and when a Baltimore columnist observed that, according to his research, not one Pirate was related to another, Pops responded that he and his teammates had a "closeness" akin to family, that "we scratched and clawed together." *Slugged* and *stifled* are verbs more appropriate to what they did to the Baltimore Orioles in this Series. After trailing three games to one, the Pirates swept the final three games, limiting Baltimore to just two runs while they scored 15. They thus became only the fourth team in Series history to come from so far behind after four games. Pops Stargell hit .400 with seven runs scored, seven batted in, four doubles and three homers. His 25 total bases set a Series record and made him the obvious choice for the Most Valuable Player award. But four other family members had 10 or more hits, and second baseman Phil Garner batted an even .500, tying him with Pepper Martin (1931) and Johnny Lindell (1947) for the highest average in a seven-game Series.

GAME 1
BALTIMORE 5, PITTSBURGH 4
GAME 2
PITTSBURGH 3, BALTIMORE 2
GAME 3
BALTIMORE 8, PITTSBURGH 4
GAME 4
BALTIMORE 9, PITTSBURGH 6
GAME 5
PITTSBURGH 7, BALTIMORE 1
GAME 6
PITTSBURGH 4, BALTIMORE 0
GAME 7
PITTSBURGH 4, BALTIMORE 1

Most of the games were played in abominable weather. The opener, in Baltimore, was postponed a day by snow, setting another Series record. It was a scarcely balmy 47° when the teams did play the next day. Game 3, in Pittsburgh, was delayed for 67 minutes by rain. Game 4, played in the damp and the cold, lasted three hours and 48 minutes, the longest nine-inning game up to that point in Series history. Game 5 was played in freezing temperatures. It was only when the two teams returned to Baltimore for Games 6 and 7 that a facsimile of baseball weather returned. It didn't help the chilled-out Orioles.

Their ace, Jim Palmer, could not keep the Family in line in the sixth game as Pittsburgh starter John Candelaria and the gaunt, sidearming reliever Kent Tekulve combined for a 4–0 shutout. In Game 7, second baseman Rich Dauer gave the Orioles hope with a third-inning solo homer off Jim Bibby. But in the sixth inning Stargell hit a two-run shot over the rightfield fence to give the Pirates a lead they would never lose. Oriole rightfielder Ken Singleton climbed the wall in vain pursuit of Pops' drive, and after it sailed into the void, he hung there for a moment, miserably clinging to the top of the wall, a living symbol of his team's plight. Tekulve again closed out the victory, his third save of the Series.

In a final family note, a sad one, Pirate manager Chuck Tanner's mother, Anne, died the morning of Game 5, the very start of his team's final drive to the championship.

STARGELL WAS THE PATERFAMILIAS OF THE PIRATES AS WELL AS THE MVP OF THE SERIES.

A SOLID PELTING—FROM THE SKIES AND FROM THE BALTIMORE BATS—UNDID CANDELARIA IN
THE THIRD GAME, BUT HE CAME BACK WITH A BRILLIANT PERFOMANCE IN GAME 6; STARGELL (RIGHT)
WAS A PROUD PAPA AFTER HIS TEAM'S SERIES-CLINCHING VICTORY IN GAME 7.

1 9 7 9

Pittsburgh / Baltimore

1 9 8 5

Kansas City Royals : 4

St. Louis Cardinals : 3

THIS SO-CALLED I-70 SERIES, "THE WAR WITHIN THE state" between the two Missouri teams developed into one of the most turbulent in history. But when seemingly all around them were losing their heads, the Royals kept theirs firmly in place and calmly won the day. They got off to a horrendous start, however, losing the first two games at home and leaving the Cardinals with the likely prospect of closing out the Series in St. Louis. As the Royals were constantly reminded, no team had ever come back to win a World Series after losing the first two at home.

But manager Dick Howser's team was nothing if not resilient. They won Game 3, 6–1, behind the six-hit pitching of Bret Saberhagen, and split the next two. Still, the Cardinals had only to win one game in Kansas City to bring the trophy across state. And they were leading 1–0 going into the last half of the ninth inning. That's when all hell broke loose.

With the two managers juggling lefty-righty pitchers and pinch hitters even before a pitch was thrown, the Royals' Jorge Orta, a lefthanded hitter, wound up leading off against Cardinal righthander Todd Worrell, who had struck out six straight Royals in Game 5. Orta looked to be overmatched. But he did manage to nub a slow roller off the end of his bat to Jack Clark at first base. Clark fielded the ball

GAME 1
ST. LOUIS 3, KANSAS CITY 1
GAME 2
ST. LOUIS 4, KANSAS CITY 2
GAME 3
KANSAS CITY 6, ST. LOUIS 1
GAME 4
ST. LOUIS 3, KANSAS CITY 0
GAME 5
KANSAS CITY 6, ST. LOUIS 1
GAME 6
KANSAS CITY 2, ST. LOUIS 1
GAME 7
KANSAS CITY 11, ST. LOUIS 0

cleanly and tossed to Worrell covering in what seemed ample time to catch the runner. But umpire Don Denkinger called Orta safe. Cardinal manager Whitey Herzog stormed out of the dugout to protest, and television replays showed convincingly that the call was wrong. But it was not changed.

The next hitter, Steve Balboni, then hit a pop foul near the first base dugout that Clark lost sight of and allowed to drop untouched. Balboni then singled and, with pinch-hitter Hal McRae at bat, Cardinal catcher Darrell Porter let a Worrell slider get by him for a passed ball, the runners advancing to second and third. Herzog ordered McRae intentionally walked. Then, with the bases loaded, pinch hitter Dane Iorg singled to right, scoring the winning runs. "It's a situation you dream about as a child," Iorg said afterward.

Denkinger's call and the last-inning rally seemed to unnerve the Cardinals, and they were blown out 11–0 in the seventh game as Saberhagen pitched his second masterpiece. In a six-run fifth inning, both Herzog and pitcher Joaquin Andujar were ejected for vehemently—nay, violently—arguing balls and strikes. The ejector was, of course, Denkinger. It was the first time both a manager and a player had been tossed out of a World Series game in 50 years. The Cardinals blamed their defeat on Denkinger, but, in truth, they had no one to blame but themselves. They hit a Series alltime low .185 for seven games and scored a total of only 13 runs.

As Kansas City's George Brett said afterward, employing an old Missouri expression, "We showed 'em."

GAMES 3 AND 7 WERE BOTH MASTERPIECES FOR THE 21-YEAR OLD SABERHAGEN.

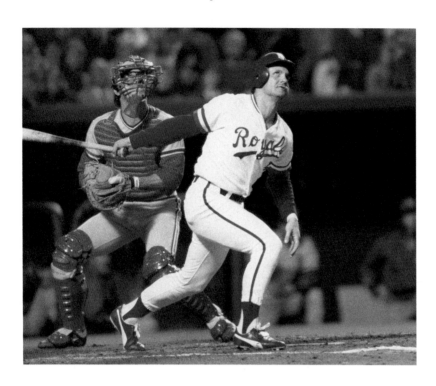

BRETT (ABOVE LEFT) LED ALL SERIES BATTERS WITH 10 HITS; DENKINGER'S MISSED CALL
IN GAME 6 (ABOVE) SEEMED TO UNNERVE THE CARDINALS IN GAME 7 AS BOTH ANDUJAR (LEFT,
BEING RESTRAINED) AND HERZOG WERE EJECTED FOR ARGUING BALLS AND STRIKES.

1 9 8 6

New York Mets : 4

Boston Red Sox : 3

TWICE IN THE BOTTOM OF THE 10TH INNING OF the sixth game, the Red Sox were but one strike away from winning their first World Series since 1918 and banishing the curse that had plagued them in the near misses of 1975, '67 and '46. Alas, they are still waiting for that third strike in New England. And of all the might-have-beens, this was the most grievous. It also added another alltime goat to the Series herd.

The Sox were ahead three games to two and leading 5–3, going into the bottom of the 10th in Game 6 at New York's Shea Stadium, having broken a tie in their own half of the inning on Dave Henderson's homer and Marty Barrett's run-scoring single. Their closer, Calvin Schiraldi, was on the mound, and he quickly retired Wally Backman and Keith Hernandez on fly balls to the outfield. But the next two hitters, Gary Carter and pinch-hitter Kevin Mitchell both singled. Schiraldi worked Ray Knight to a two-strike count but then lost him to a bloop single to center, which scored Carter. Manager John McNamara then lifted Schiraldi and brought in the veteran Bob Stanley to pitch to switch-hitting Mookie Wilson. Normally a wild swinger, Wilson was determined in this critical situation to have a quality at bat. He certainly did.

GAME 1
BOSTON 1, NEW YORK 0
GAME 2
BOSTON 9, NEW YORK 3
GAME 3
NEW YORK 7, BOSTON 1
GAME 4
NEW YORK 6, BOSTON 2
GAME 5
BOSTON 4, NEW YORK 2
GAME 6
NEW YORK 6, BOSTON 5
GAME 7
NEW YORK 8, BOSTON 5

The count on him went 0 and 1, 1 and 1, 2 and 1, then 2 and 2. One strike away. Wilson fouled off two breaking balls. Stanley planned to finish him off with a fastball inside, but the pitch got away from him and headed for Wilson's rib cage. If the ball had hit him, the bases would have been loaded, but Wilson instinctively leaped aside, momentarily blocking the view of Boston catcher Rich Gedman. The ball sailed past Gedman to the backstop for a wild pitch, and Mitchell, answering third base coach Bud Harrelson's pleas of "Go, go, go!" steamed home with the tying run.

The count was now 3 and 2. Wilson fouled off two more pitches. On the next, he drove a medium-speed roller toward Bill Buckner at first base. The third out at last! But no. The ball, said Buckner later, "bounced and bounced, and then it didn't bounce. It skipped." Right through his injured legs, as Knight fairly flew home from third with the winning and Series-tying run.

The Red Sox got a little time to recover from this calamity when Game 7 was postponed a day because of rain. But it wasn't enough. The Mets, trailing 3–0 in the early going, exploded in the final three innings against a tired Bruce Hurst, trying for his third Series victory, and five successors, including Schiraldi and Stanley, to win 8–5 and plunge all of New England into its customary autumnal gloom.

"I can't remember the last time I missed a ground ball," Buckner lamented. "I'll remember that one." So will a lot of other people.

KEITH HERNANDEZ (RIGHT ABOVE), A TEAM LEADER THROUGHOUT THE SEASON, DROVE IN FOUR
RUNS IN THE SERIES; DARRYL STRAWBERRY (RIGHT) BROKE OUT OF A SERIES SLUMP WITH A HOME
RUN IN GAME 7; RELIEVER JESSE OROSCO CELEBRATED THE FINAL OUT IN HIGH STYLE.

1986

New York / Boston

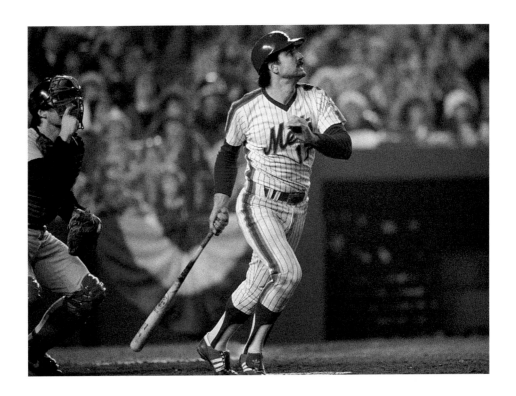

1991

THIS CINDERELLA SERIES BETWEEN TWO TEAMS that finished last the year before is another that could lay just claim to being the best ever. Five of the seven games were decided by one run, three of them in extra innings and four in the home half of the final inning. It introduced an array of unknown heroes. Minnesota third baseman Scott Leius won the second game with an eighth-inning homer. Atlanta second baseman Mark Lemke, a career .225 hitter, won the third game with a 12th-inning single and scored the winning run in the fourth game after hitting a triple, the first of three he belted in the Series. And the whole shebang came down to a last at bat by Minnesota utilityman Gene Larkin. Most of all, though, this Series finished with two of the most tense and thrilling games ever played on the big stage.

GAME 1
MINNESOTA 5, ATLANTA 2
GAME 2
MINNESOTA 3, ATLANTA 2
GAME 3
ATLANTA 5, MINNESOTA 4
GAME 4
ATLANTA 3, MINNESOTA 2
GAME 5
ATLANTA 14, MINNESOTA 5
GAME 6
MINNESOTA 4, ATLANTA 3
GAME 7
MINNESOTA 1, ATLANTA 0

The Braves, winners of all three games in Atlanta after losing the first two at Minneapolis, were trying to finish things off in the inhospitable Metrodome. They were greeted by a revived Kirby Puckett. A .167 hitter in the first five games, Puckett had already hit a single, a triple and a sacrifice fly, stolen a base and made a brilliant catch before coming to bat as the leadoff hitter against Charlie Leibrandt in the 11th inning with the score tied 3–3. Then, in a moment reminiscent of Carlton Fisk's climactic clout in Game 6 of 1975, Puckett hit Leibrandt's fourth pitch into the left centerfield bleachers to send his team roaring into a seventh game.

The best was saved for last. With Minnesota's Jack Morris and Atlanta's John Smoltz pitching superbly, the two teams were scoreless through seven innings. Then, in the Atlanta half of the eighth, Lonnie Smith, playing in his fourth World Series for his fourth different team, led off with a single. The next hitter, Terry Pendleton, poked a long drive off the fence in left center. Smith, running with the pitch, never saw the ball, and when Atlanta infielders Lemke and Chuck Knoblauch decoyed him with a fake fielding play, he paused at second base. Then he saw the ball in the outfield. Too late. He was only able to reach third on the long double, a costly blunder since he was still on third when a bases-loaded double play ended the inning.

And so they battled on to the 10th inning, Smoltz gone by now, Morris still pitching goose eggs. Dan Gladden led off the home half with a bloop double to left center. Knoblauch sacrificed him to third, and after Puckett and Kent Hrbek were intentionally walked, Twin manager Tom Kelly sent Larkin up as a pinch hitter against Atlanta reliever Alejandro Pena. Larkin hit the first pitch over a drawn-in outfield, and Gladden hopped on home plate with both feet as the Homer Hankie–waving Twin fans went wild. The Series had been so closely fought that, as Lemke suggested, perhaps seriously, "Maybe they should have just stopped this game after nine innings and cut the trophy in half." It does seem a pity someone had to lose.

MORRIS PITCHED A PAIR OF GRITTY VICTORIES, INCLUDING A 10-INNING CLASSIC IN GAME 7.

1991

Minnesota / Atlanta

GREG OLSON HELD ON FOR THE OUT, BUT GLADDEN AND THE TWINS PREVAILED IN GAME 1 ANYWAY.

Teams

Chicago Cubs
1906-08

These are the saddest of possible words:
Tinker to Evers to Chance.
Trio of bear Cubs fleeter than birds,
Tinker to Evers to Chance.
Ruthlessly pricking our gonfalon bubble,
Making a Giant hit into a double —
Words that are heavy with nothing but trouble:
Tinker to Evers to Chance.
—Franklin Pierce Adams

YES, THE THREE-TIME NATIONAL LEAGUE CHAMPION Chicago Cubs of the Edwardian Age fielded that fabled double play combination of shortstop Joe Tinker, second baseman Johnny Evers and first baseman–manager Frank Chance, the only players to enter the Hall of Fame tout ensemble. But they had much, much more, principally the intimidating pitching rotation of Mordecai (Three-Finger) Brown, Ed Reulbach, Orval Overall and John (Jack the Giant Killer) Pfiester that won 232 of the amazing 322 wins the Cubs amassed in those three unforgettable — for succeeding generations of Cub fans — seasons.

Hall of Famer Brown lost most of his index finger and paralyzed his little finger when, at age seven, he imprudently stuck his right hand into his uncle's corn shredder back home in Indiana. It must not have seemed so at the time, but professionally at least, it was the best thing that ever happened to him. Determined to play baseball despite the handicap, he developed a grip that gave him a natural sinker. His three-fingered delivery so mystified hitters that Brown won 20 or more games for six straight seasons, from 1906 through '11, and chalked up consecutive earned run averages of 1.04, 1.39, 1.47, 1.31, 1.86 and 2.80. Many a pitcher would be willing to give up much of his right hand for those staggering statistics.

The Cubs won a major league–record 116 games in 1906, finishing a full 20 games ahead of the second-place Giants but then, to the astonishment of the sporting world, lost the World Series, four games to two, to the

"Hitless Wonders" Chicago White Sox, a team that collectively batted only .230 that season, with just seven home runs. The Wonders hit only .198 in the Series, but they held the mighty Cubs to an even paltrier .196. It was the first and last all-Chicago World Series.

Smarting from this humiliating upset, the Cubs roared back with 107 wins in '07 and finished 17 games ahead of the Pirates. The first World Series game against the Detroit Tigers was called on account of darkness with the score tied 3–3 in the 12th inning. Then the Cubs methodically swept the Tigers four straight, limiting Detroit's 20-year-old sensation, Ty Cobb, to just four hits in 20 at bats. Harry Steinfeldt, the forgotten man at third base in baseball's most celebrated infield, hit a resounding .471 for Chicago. Of the Cubs' 43 hits, 36 were singles. But this was a team that prospered on pitching, speed and defense, not slugging. The Cubs stole 18 bases in this Series, and the four victories were equally divided among the four starters.

The next year was no cakewalk. In fact, the Cubs might not have gotten into the Series at all had it not been for Fred Merkle's legendary base path boner of September 23. Merkle, on first base when Al Bridwell hit an apparent game-winning single for the Giants, ran directly to the Polo Grounds clubhouse instead of first touching second base. But Evers, amid mass confusion, called for the ball from the outfield, somehow got it, or a reasonable facsimile, and stepped on second for what umpire Hank O'Day ruled a force-out. The game was called a tie and replayed on October 8 after the Giants and Cubs finished in a dead heat at the end of the regular season. Brown, pitching in relief, beat the Giants' Christy Mathewson 4–2 for the pennant.

The Cubs once again crushed the Tigers in the Series, four games to one this time, winning so convincingly that only 6,210 fans, the smallest crowd in World Series history, turned out at Detroit's Bennett Park to watch Overall shut out the home team 2–0 in the fifth and final game.

It was, of course, the last World Series the Cubs would ever win.

Philadelphia A's
1910-14

CONNIE MACK BELIEVED IN SMART ballplayers, and so it was that his first great team had a halls of ivy look to it. Star pitchers Eddie Plank (Gettysburg), Chief Bender (Carlisle) and Jack Coombs (Colby) were all collegians and so were two members of the "$100,000 Infield," Eddie Collins (Columbia) and Jack Barry (Holy Cross). Contrary to conventional baseball wisdom of the time, brains proved to be no handicap as these academic Philadelphia Athletics won four American League pennants and three World Series in five years. And three of the college boys—Plank, Bender and Collins—graduated to baseball's Hall of Fame.

In the 1910 World Series, the sis-boom-bah kids toppled the mighty Cubs, winners of four National League titles in five years, four games to one. The A's scored an average of seven runs a game and hit .316, the highest team average in a Series until the Yankees batted .338 in losing to the Pirates 50 years later. Plank had a sore arm and was unable to pitch, so Mack went with just two starters. Bender won the opener 4–1 and lost the fourth game to Three-Finger Brown 4–3. Coombs won the rest: 9–3 on October 18, 12–5 on October 20 and 7–2 on October 23. He even contributed a pair of RBIs in the Game 3 victory. It was a most remarkable performance in what was a remarkable career. In the four previous seasons Coombs had won only 35 games. In 1910 he won 31 and followed that with 28 wins in '11 and 21 in '12. Then, beset by injuries, he would not win another game until 1915, with Brooklyn, and only 44 more for the remainder of his 14-year career.

In 1911 the famous $100,000 Infield was completed with the emergence of 21-year-old John Phalen (Stuffy) McInnis as the regular first baseman. He joined Collins at second, Barry at short and Frank (Home Run) Baker at third. McInnis hit .321 in '11 and .327, .326 and .314

in the next three seasons for Mack. But the '11 Series not only belonged to Baker, it gave him his timeless nickname, as the Athletics dispatched the Giants four games to two.

The A's won 90 games in 1912 but finished 15 back of the Red Sox, to whom they loaned the pennant for a year. In 1913 the A's were back stronger than ever, finishing 6½ games ahead of the Senators. And in the Series they beat John McGraw's Giants again, four games to one, the only loss a shutout by the apparently impregnable Christy Mathewson in Game 2. The fidgety Plank—he talked to the ball more than 60 years before Mark Fidrych ever thought of it—beat Mathewson in the fifth and final game, 3–1. Mack used just 12 players in the entire Series—two catchers besides the position players and three pitchers, Bender, Plank and 21-year-old "Bullet Joe" Bush, who won the third game 8–2. Baker again starred at the plate, hitting .450 with another home run and a Series-leading seven runs batted in. Collins was not far behind at .421.

The Athletics had lost only four games in the three previous Series, but in a shocking upset they were swept in 1914 by the Miracle Braves of Hank Gowdy and Rabbit Maranville. The losses went to Plank, Bush, Bob Shawkey and, after a record six Series victories, to Bender. Mack was so disheartened by this sudden and unexpected collapse and so strapped for cash that he broke up his own team, selling or trading off most of his stars, a move that would be reprised 60 years later by Charlie Finley, another A's owner who dismantled a baseball dynasty. The stripped-down Athletics of 1915 won only 43 games and finished last, the first in a string of seven straight cellar-dwelling years. It would be another 15 years before Mack would field another pennant winner.

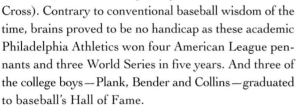

Champions 1910

Philadelphia (Athletic) Base Ball Club
American League

THE A'S (ABOVE) INCLUDED BAKER, WHO TOOK A SERIES SPIKING FROM FRED SNODGRASS IN 1911 (INSET LEFT).

New York Giants
1917-24

THE ONCE PROUD GIANTS HIT BOTTOM IN 1915 WITH A last-place finish, then climbed to fourth in '16 and first in '17. But they lost the Series that year to the Chicago White Sox, and when Sox manager Clarence (Pants) Rowland sought to commiserate with John McGraw, the acerbic Giant skipper responded, none too graciously, "Get away from me, you busher!" It was a measure of the frustration McGraw was experiencing in this relatively fallow period before he put together his finest teams. Interest in his team had so declined that the second-place Giants drew only 256,000 to the Polo Grounds in the war-shortened season of 1918. Then in 1919, Charles A. Stoneham, a stockholder with Tammany Hall and racetrack connections, became the majority owner and team president, and the good times started to roll. And none too soon, for the Giants' Polo Grounds tenants, the orphan Yankees, were becoming a genuine threat to take over the big town.

McGraw, who hobnobbed with Broadway sharpies and theater people, regarded the Yanks with undisguised contempt. Why, they didn't even know how to play the game scientifically, depending on some kid named Ruth to hit the ball out of the lot. The kid was, in fact, revolutionizing the game, and McGraw never forgave him for it. Ruth hit 54 home runs in 1920 and 59 in '21 when the Yankees and Giants met in the first Series played in one ballpark, the Polo Grounds. McGraw had the sort of team he liked, speedy and sharp defensively. The acquisition of second baseman Johnny Rawlings from Philadelphia (he came with an outfielder named Casey Stengel) obliged him to shift Frankie Frisch from second to third, but the Fordham Flash could play anywhere. And with Dave (Beauty) Bancroft at short and George (Highpockets) Kelly at first, the Giants were airtight in the infield. And they beat the Yankees five games to three, the Babe retiring from the fray after the fifth game with an abscessed elbow. Afterward McGraw boasted that it was his pitch calling that silenced Ruth, although the Babe wasn't that quiet, hitting .313 with a homer and four RBIs.

McGraw had more reason to crow in 1922 when his Giants swept the despised Yankees in four games, the Series having returned to the best four-of-seven format favored by commissioner Kenesaw Mountain Landis. Ruth was an embarrassing 2 for 17 in this one, with only one RBI. The press was now calling the Giants' manager "Little Napoleon" and hailing him as the game's greatest strategist. Lapping it up, McGraw celebrated long and hard afterward with his Broadway pals.

In 1923 the two New York teams met for a third time but with drastically different results. For one thing, the Yankees had moved into their own magnificent stadium, the House that Ruth Built, across the Harlem River, and though the Polo Grounds had been expanded to seat 52,000, Yankee Stadium seemed to dwarf it. McGraw so detested the new park that he refused to allow his players to dress there, insisting that they change into their uniforms in the Polo Grounds and then travel across the river, like the French army defending Paris in the recently concluded Great War, in a fleet of taxicabs.

The Giants won the first game at the new park when Stengel broke up a 4–4 tie in the ninth with an inside-the-park home run sliced into the vast alley in left centerfield. It was the Giants' eighth straight win over their now cross-river rivals, and it prompted McGraw to remark carelessly, "Why shouldn't we pitch to Ruth? We pitch to better hitters than Ruth in the National League."

"Ere the sun had set on McGraw's rash and impetuous words," wrote columnist Heywood Broun, than "the Babe had flashed across the sky fiery portents which should have been sufficient to strike terror and conviction in the hearts of all infidels." Ruth, in fact, hit two towering home runs the very next day, and the Yanks were off to their first Series victory, four games to two. Attendance at Yankee Stadium for the third game reached 62,430, the largest crowd ever to see a major league baseball game … until two days later when 62,817 showed up there.

McGraw, alas, never won another Series.

New York Yankees
1926-32

THE 1923 WORLD SERIES WIN BY THE NEW YORK YANKEES presaged the greatest dynasty in the history of American sports. Between 1921, their first appearance, and '64, the Yankees never had to wait longer than four years for a championship. From their first World Series to their last, in 1996, they won 23 world titles and an unequaled total of 113 World Series games. No other team in either league has ever won more than nine World Series, and the next highest total of games won is 48. And this astonishing record has its beginnings in the team most analysts still consider to be the best that baseball has ever given us.

The Yankees' loss to the Cardinals in 1926, their third in four World Series appearances, set this proud team aflame. It's pure speculation, of course, to rank the 1927 team with its "Murderers' Row" as the best ever, but a sound enough argument can surely be advanced in its behalf. The '27 Yanks won 110 games, an American League record that would survive for 27 years. The team batting average was .307, its slugging percentage an alltime record .489. The Yankees hit 158 home runs that year, 102 more than their closest competitors, the Athletics, in the American League. Babe Ruth alone out-homered every other team in the league with his record 60. Ruth hit .356 that year with 164 RBIs and a league-leading 158 runs scored. Lou Gehrig batted .373 and hit 47 homers, 18 triples and 52 doubles. He scored 149 runs and batted in a league-record 175. Ruth's slugging percentage was .772, the third highest percentage ever; Gehrig's .765 was fourth alltime. The heart of Murderers' Row—Ruth, Gehrig, Bob Meusel and Tony Lazzeri—all drove in more than 100 runs. Leadoff hitter Earle Combs averaged .356 and led the league with 231 hits. In fact, a Yankee was at the top of the league leaders' list in virtually every offensive category, including runs (Ruth), hits (Combs), doubles (Gehrig), triples (Combs), home runs (Ruth), total bases (Gehrig), RBIs (Gehrig), bases on balls (Ruth), on base percentage

(Ruth), and slugging percentage (Ruth). Even the defensive specialists, shortstop Mark Koenig and third baseman Jumping Joe Dugan, hit well, Koenig averaging .285, Dugan .269.

And the pitching wasn't bad either. Waite Hoyt led the league with 22 wins and a 2.63 earned run average. Herb Pennock, another Connie Mack castoff, was 19–8 in his 15th big league season. Urban Shocker, one of seven remaining legal spitballers, was 18–6, and Wiley Moore, a 30-year-old rookie who fluctuated between the rotation and the bullpen, was 19–7 with, according to modern rules, 13 saves.

Legend has it that in '27 the Yankees so awed their World Series opponents, the Pirates, by crashing batting practice pitches out of Forbes Field before the first game that the outcome was resolved before a pitch was thrown. Legend aside, the Yanks did sweep Pittsburgh with Koenig hitting .500 for the four games and Ruth .400 with a pair of homers and seven RBIs. Even the great Pie Traynor seemed cowed by the Yankee might, hitting just .200 and failing to drive in a single run. The Cardinals got more of the same the next year, the Yankees scoring their second successive sweep and gaining blessed revenge for the Series of '26. Ruth hit .625 in this one, with three homers, all in the fourth game, and nine runs scored. Gehrig batted .545 with five runs scored and nine driven in. Four of his six hits were homers.

The Yankees had to wait until 1932 for their next World Series appearance, but again they won in four straight, this time over the Cubs. That added up to 12 consecutive World Series wins. But this one was overshadowed by Ruth's alleged "called shot," a grand gesture that also took the play away from Gehrig's .529 average, three home runs and eight RBIs in the four games.

The Age of Ruth would soon pass, only to be replaced by the Age of DiMaggio. To the rest of baseball, there was seemingly no end to Yankee domination.

RUTH (LEFT) AND GEHRIG: THE TOWERING PILLARS OF PERHAPS THE GREATEST TEAM EVER.

St. Louis Cardinals
1928-34

CARDINALS OWNER SAM BREADON WAS SO DEMORAL-ized by the Yankees' demolition of his team in the 1928 Series that he fired manager Bill McKechnie only a few weeks afterward. This was hardly an act of unprece-dented impulsiveness, for Breadon had also fired Rogers Hornsby as manager and traded him as a player after the Cardinals had won the 1926 Series, the team's first cham-pionship. This time he demoted McKechnie to the Rochester farm team and brought up that club's manag-er, Billy Southworth, to lead the Cardinals in 1929. But Breadon soon became disenchanted with the authoritarian Southworth and flip-flopped him with McKechnie in midseason. McKechnie, once more unto the breech, sur-vived only until the end of the 1929 season, when he was replaced by Gabby Street. Counting Bob O'Farrell, who managed in 1927 after Hornsby's sacking, the Cardi-nals had five managers in five seasons while winning three pennants and a World Series.

Street, best known as a Senator catcher who caught a ball dropped from the Washington Monument, actually hung around long enough to win pennants in 1930 and '31 and, thanks to the daring of Pepper Martin, a World Series in '31. The '31 Cards finished 13 games ahead in the National League and then upset Connie Mack's powerful Athletics in the Series, avenging the loss of the year before. Four of these Cards—first baseman Sunny Jim Bottomley, second baseman Frankie Frisch, outfielder Chick Hafey and pitcher Burleigh Grimes— would be elected to the Hall of Fame.

Street survived until early in the 1933 season, when Breadon replaced him with Frisch, who was acquired from the Giants in the Hornsby trade of 1926. Frisch, a spec-tacular all-around player, had a simple philosophy as manager: "A man is up to bat four times a day as a rule. He's out there from two to five. Why can't he hustle? Why won't he run out everything? The fans don't like to see a guy joggin' down to first and maybe carrying his bat with him. That looks lousy."

Frisch had no trouble convincing his '34 team, the famous Gashouse Gang, to hustle. Probably no team in baseball history hustled harder than the roustabouts Frisch sent out to play that fabulous season. And they were equally active off the field, setting off firecrackers in hotel lobbies, spraying sneeze powder in crowded buses and subways, dropping water bags from upper-story windows on unsuspecting pedestrians and playing pranks on everyone, including their manager. "I'll wager that no ball club ever got more fun out of playing than we did," said first baseman Ripper Collins. "It wasn't that we broke training, because we didn't. It was merely anything for a laugh."

Frisch had his managerial hands full controlling this unruly bunch, but he couldn't fault their play. They sped past the Giants in the last weekend of the season and kept on running through the stunned Detroit Tigers in the Series, with the Dean brothers, Dizzy and Paul, winning two games apiece. Diz had a dream 30–7 season, leading the league in wins, shutouts (seven) and strikeouts (195). Paul chipped in with 19 wins, one of which was a no-hitter pitched in the second game of a double-header. Dizzy had tossed a three-hit shutout in the first game.

Sportswriters tried vainly to stick the almost somnolent Paul with the nickname Daffy, in an effort to match monickers with his brother, but the name never caught on. Besides, while Paul was shy and subdued, the elder Dean, who often staged mock fistfights with Pepper Martin in hotel lobbies, the two spitting out popcorn kernels as if they were teeth, really was dizzy. Alas, his meteoric career, like those of so many of his Gashouse teammates, would be a short one. He suffered a broken toe when hit by a line drive off the bat of Earl Averill in the 1937 All-Star Game, then tried to come back too soon and hurt his priceless arm. The blinding speed was gone forever.

This was simply a team too good and too funny to last.

New York Yankees
1936-43

AFTER SUFFERING THE RARE HUMILIATION OF THREE straight second-place finishes, the Yankees reemerged in 1936 with a team to rival the previously incomparable Murderers' Row for all-around excellence. And then they quietly built on that solid base, adding in successive years rookies Tommy Henrich (1937), Joe Gordon ('38) and Charlie Keller ('39). By the end of the '39 season, the cry "Break up the Yankees" was heard throughout the baseball land. As it turned out, only World War II could do that.

The first rookie added to the Yankee mix was one who transformed an also-ran into the invincible Bronx Bombers—a 21-year-old centerfielder from San Francisco named Joe DiMaggio. In his last year with the San Francisco Seals of the Pacific Coast League, DiMaggio had hit .398. Two years earlier, at age 18, he had put together a portentous 61-game hitting streak. He arrived at Yankee Stadium with as much fanfare as any rookie in the game's history, then promptly missed the first 17 games of the season with a foot injury. He did not disappoint thereafter, though, hitting .323 with 29 homers and 125 RBIs in his first season.

DiMaggio ignited an already powerful team led by Lou Gehrig, who at age 33 enjoyed one of his finest years, batting .354 with 152 RBIs and tying his career high with 49 homers. Larrupin' Lou's roommate, the veteran catcher Bill Dickey, hit .362 with 22 homers and 107 RBIs. The peerless second baseman, Tony Lazzeri, also drove in 107 runs.

The pitching staff was anchored by Red Ruffing and the droll Vernon (Lefty) Gomez, who claimed credit for DiMaggio's emergence as the game's best centerfielder. "Until I pitched," El Goofo remarked, "they never knew he could go back on a ball." Between 1930—when Ruffing joined the team and Gomez came up as a rookie—and 1942, these two Hall of Famers combined for 408 wins.

The '36 Yanks had 102 wins, clinched the pennant by September 9, the earliest yet, and beat the Giants in the Series, four games to two, in the first Subway Series

since 1923. The two teams met again in '37, and the Yankees won even more convincingly, taking the first three games by scores of 8–1, 8–1 and 5–1 and, after a loss to King Carl Hubbell, winning the finale 4–2 behind Gomez. This would be the last Series for Lazzeri, a link to the '27 team, as a Yankee, and he signed off with a .400 average. "Poosh-'em-up-Tony" would return to the Fall Classic the next year as a Chicago Cub and watch, mostly from the bench, as his old team, strengthened by Gordon, his replacement at second base, swept the Series.

The 1939 Yankees may well have been the equal of the '36 Bombers, although Gehrig, stricken with amyotrophic lateral sclerosis, the lethal disease that would thereafter bear his name, was sadly absent. Charlie (King Kong) Keller joined DiMaggio and Henrich to form baseball's best outfield and hit .334 as a rookie and .438 in the Series. Third baseman Red Rolfe, an unassuming Ivy Leaguer from Dartmouth, had his best of a succession of very good years, hitting .329 and leading the league in hits (213), doubles (46) and runs scored (139). The '39 team won 106 games, finished 17 ahead of the Red Sox and scored a second straight Series sweep, this time over Cincinnati. "Break up the Yankees!"

In 1941, the year of DiMaggio's 56-game hitting streak, the Yanks returned to the Series after a one-year hiatus and thanks in no small part to Dodger catcher Mickey Owen's third strike muff, took Brooklyn in five games. It was a year in which the outfielders, DiMag, Henrich and King Kong, all hit 30 or more homers. The Yankees lost to the speedy Cardinals in '42, but avenged that loss in '43 with both Henrich and DiMaggio, among others, in the service, whipping the Cards in five games. Spurgeon (Spud) Chandler, who had a sensational 20–4 season in '43, pitched two complete game wins, the last a shutout.

It had been quite a run for the Bombers—six pennants and five world championships in seven seasons—but they would tuck it in for the duration and come back with a quite different, if even more successful, team after the war.

New York Yankees
1949-51

FORD WAS ALL SMILES AFTER HIS
FIRST SERIES WIN IN 1950.

THERE WAS LITTLE TO SUGGEST that this 1949 team would launch a new Yankee dynasty, one that would even surpass in Series victories the powerhouses that preceded it in the 1920s and '30s. This team batted a mere .269, nearly 30 percentage points below Murderers' Row. It hit only 115 home runs. The Yankees of 1936 through '39 averaged 174 homers a season. Instead of finishing nearly 20 games ahead of its nearest competitor, this team won the pennant on the last day of the season. And as opposed to the worrywart Miller Huggins and the solemn "Marse Joe" McCarthy, these Yankees were managed by a clown.

In nine previous seasons as a big league manager, with the Brooklyn Dodgers and Boston Braves, Casey Stengel had never finished out of the second division. But he had impressed Yankee general manager George Weiss by taking an Oakland team of mostly big league retreads — the "Nine Old Men" — and one youngster, Billy Martin, to the Pacific Coast League championship in 1948. Stengel had done it by crafty platooning of the daily players and masterful manipulation of an aging pitching staff. Weiss was impressed, but few others in the Yankee organization were until the G.M. convinced co-owner Del Webb that Stengel was the man to replace the popular Bucky Harris, who in two years at the helm had won one pennant and narrowly missed another. Stengel took over to mostly jeers from the public. He was nearly 59 years old.

And he had nothing but trouble his first year. Joe DiMaggio missed the first 65 games with bone spurs on his heel, then returned with a typical flourish in late June by demolishing the Red Sox in a three-game series with four homers and nine RBIs at Fenway Park. The Yankee Clipper hit .346 for the rest of the season, with 14 homers and 67 RBIs in only 272 times at bat. Charlie Keller would be limited to pinch-hitting that season because of a bad back and Tommy

Henrich would be forced to abandon rightfield to play first base. Henrich was able to return to the outfield late in the season when the Yanks acquired Johnny Mize from the Giants, but Mize hadn't been with the team a week before he suffered a separated shoulder.

And yet the Yanks edged the Red Sox in a nail-biting pennant race and beat the Dodgers, four games to one, in the Series. They won Stengel style, with platooning — mainly with outfielders Hank Bauer and Gene Woodling — and superior pitching. For starters the Yankees had Allie Reynolds, Vic Raschi and Eddie Lopat, and in the bullpen the redoubtable lefty Joe Page. The Yanks swept the Phillies' Whiz Kids in the 1950 Series, the franchise's sixth sweep and 13th world title. The already formidable staff was measurably improved with the addition of young Whitey Ford, who, after being called up from Kansas City on June 29, won nine straight games before losing in relief on September 27. Ford pitched 8⅔ innings in his only Series start, in Game 4. It would be the first of a record 10 World Series wins.

DiMaggio played his last game in the 1951 Series, closing out, at age 36, a legendary career on a winning note, driving in five runs as the Yankees again beat the Giants, four games to two. The Polo Grounders came into the Series fresh from Bobby Thomson's "Shot Heard 'round the World" homer that beat the Dodgers in the National League playoff, and they won two of the first three games. But a rainout after Game 3 gave Stengel time to regroup his tired pitching corps and halt the Giants' charge.

DiMaggio's successor in centerfield, the 19-year-old Mickey Mantle, was injured in the second game when he stepped on a drain cover at Yankee Stadium and strained his right knee. Like his illustrious predecessor, Mantle's magnificent career would be marred and eventually cut short, at age 37, by a succession of injuries.

MONTE IRVIN WATCHES GIL McDOUGALD'S HOME RUN DEPART THE POLO GROUNDS IN 1951'S GAME 5.

New York Yankees
1952-64

THESE WOULD BE THE FINAL YEARS OF NEARLY FOUR decades of Yankee dominance. In 1952 Casey Stengel would tie Joe McCarthy by managing his fourth straight world champion, beating the Dodgers four games to three. Twenty-year-old Mickey Mantle would hit the first of his record 18 World Series homers, and 39-year-old Johnny Mize would blast three homers, but second baseman Billy Martin would save the Series with a fielding play. The bases were loaded with two outs in the seventh inning of the seventh game and the Yankees leading 4–2, when Jackie Robinson lofted an easy pop-up near the mound that somehow left pitcher Bob Kuzava transfixed, catcher Yogi Berra confused and first baseman Joe Collins blinded by the late afternoon sun at Ebbets Field. Martin, realizing with horror that none of the three was going to catch the ball and that Dodger base runners, off with the pitch, were pounding toward home, charged in at the last second and made the game-saving catch at his shoe tops.

Stengel passed McCarthy the next year with his fifth consecutive title, defeating a great Brooklyn team, four games to two. It was the seventh loss in seven Series for the Dodgers, dating to 1916, and their fifth in a row to the hated Yankees. It was also the American League's 33rd win in the 50 Series to date. Martin again plagued the Boys of Summer, batting .500 and driving in eight runs, including the Series-winner in Game 6 with his 12th hit. The Dodgers would break their Series losing streak two years later, whipping the Yanks, four games to three, after losing the first two. In '56 the Yanks would respond in kind as Don Larsen pitched to perfection in Game 5, and a fabulous late-season acquisition, Enos Slaughter, hit a three-run homer in Game 3 and batted .350 for the Series.

The Yanks would also trade seven-game Series with the Milwaukee Braves in 1957 and '58, Stengel tying McCarthy in '58 with seven total postseason wins. The 70-year-old Case would get one more chance to surpass Marse Joe in 1960, but the Yankees, despite hitting .338 as a team, would lose to the Pirates on Bill Mazeroski's ninth-inning homer in Game 7. Stengel's replacement, 41-year-old Ralph Houk, shared none of the old man's passion for lineup shuffling. Not that he had any need to tinker with a team, led by Mantle and Roger Maris, that hit an alltime record 240 home runs.

Maris himself committed the apparently unpardonable sin of passing Babe Ruth with his 61st homer in 1961, off Boston rookie Tracy Stallard in the 162nd game of an expanded season. Purists argued that Maris's record was bogus since Ruth's 60 were hit in 154 games and Roger had prospered on pitching diluted by the addition of expansion teams in the Twin Cities and Los Angeles. The poor man's crewcut hair began to fall out in clumps under the pressure and the carping. Mantle, meanwhile, whacked 54 homers on his own and might have been even more of a threat to the Babe had he not suffered from a hip infection late in the season that limited him to just two games in a World Series the Yanks won from the Reds, four games to one.

The Yankees beat the now San Francisco Giants four games to three in 1962, as Ralph Terry, loser in four straight Classics, pitched a 1–0 shutout at Candlestick Park in the seventh game, second baseman Bobby Richardson gloving Willie McCovey's searing line drive for the final out with the winning runs on base. But there were hard times ahead. Dodger pitching swept the Yanks in '63, and the Cardinals beat them, four games to three, in '64, their manager, Johnny Keane, quitting afterward to sign on as the new Yankee manager. He replaced Berra, fired after his only season as manager, a pennant winner. It was Yogi's 15th World Series with New York either as a player or manager, Mantle's 12th and last, Ford's 11th and last. It was the Yankees' 15th Series—10 of them victorious—in 18 postwar seasons.

It was also the end of an era. After never being obliged to wait more than four years to get into one, the once proud Bombers would not make it back to the World Series until another 11 seasons had passed.

BERRA, GIL MCDOUGALD (15) AND HANK BAUER (9) GREETED MANTLE AFTER HIS HOMER IN 1953'S GAME 2.

Brooklyn Dodgers
1952-56

YOU WONDER WHAT TOOK THEM SO LONG. THESE, AFTER all, were author Roger Kahn's famous Boys of Summer, star-studded and star-crossed teams that, were it not for those spoilsports in the Bronx, would have been baseball's best team for the better part of a decade. It's just that, for the life of them, they couldn't beat the Yankees in the games that counted. In 1952 rookie Joe Black, a 15-game winner mostly in relief, pitched a six-hit win in Game 1 of the Series; Preacher Roe, 11–2 that year, won the third game; and Carl Erskine (14–6) won the fifth, but the Yanks, led by Mickey Mantle, Johnny Mize and Vic Raschi, won the rest.

In '53 the Boys may have fielded their best team. They won 105 games, hit 208 homers and scored 955 runs. Centerfielder Duke Snider batted .336, hit 42 homers, drove in 126 runs and scored a league-leading 132. National League Most Valuable Player Roy Campanella led the league with 142 RBIs and belted 41 homers. First baseman Gil Hodges hit 31 and drove in 122 runs. Jackie Robinson, now mostly an outfielder and third baseman, hit .329, and Jim (Junior) Gilliam, Robinson's replacement at second base, hit .278, scored 125 runs and led the league with 17 triples. He was voted the league's Rookie of the Year. Erskine won 20 games and lost only six, Russ Meyer won 15 and Billy Loes 14. Clem Labine won 10 games in relief, 11 overall. Preacher Roe was 11–3, giving him a record for the past three years of 44–8, a winning percentage of .846. And rookie Johnny Podres was 9–4. With Billy Cox at third, Pee Wee Reese at short, Gilliam at second and Hodges at first, the Dodgers had the best infield in all of baseball. But the '53 team could win only two games against the Yanks at October crunch time as Billy Martin went wild against the Dodger pitching staff, collecting 12 hits and driving in eight runs.

Two years later—after one anomalous season in which neither the Yankees or the Dodgers appeared in the Series, the only time between 1949 and '59 that such

MANAGER WALTER ALSTON AND THE BOYS OF SUMMER (FROM LEFT): CAMPANELLA, CARL FURILLO, HODGES, AMOROS, ROBINSON, SNIDER, REESE, GILLIAM AND MAGLIE.

heresy was allowed to occur—they would finally break the evil spell, edging their nemeses in seven difficult games. Podres won the clincher with a 2–0 shutout, his second win of the Series; Sandy Amoros, who made a sensational game-saving catch, and Snider, who whacked four home runs, provided the rest of the heroics. The next year they were back on the losing track and utterly futile against Don Larsen. More's the pity, since the old-Giant-new-Dodger Sal Maglie pitched a honey himself, retiring the first 11 Yankees. The 12th, Mickey Mantle, hit a home run. Maglie gave up one more run on a Hank Bauer single in the sixth, but that was all. He yielded only five hits and walked two. The trouble was, there was nought but zeros after Larsen's name. The Dodgers were also victimized by their best pitcher, 27-game-winner Don Newcombe, who lasted only 4⅔ innings and gave up 11 runs in his two disastrous appearances.

The 1956 Series was the Boys' last fling. Robinson, 37, would retire to the business world, disheartened as he was to learn that he had been sold across the river to the hated Giants, who in vain offered him a then generous $60,000 to play one more season. Campanella would play in '57, but on a wintry January night in 1958, his car would spin out of control on an icy Long Island road, bounce off a utility pole and flip over, crushing him against the steering wheel. The great catcher would never walk again. Reese, the team leader and impeccable shortstop, would play only another season and a half. Cox, one of the finest fielding third basemen in baseball history, was gone after '55. The world titles had been few, but the Hall of Fame inductions would be many. Reese, Snider, Campanella and Robinson would all be enshrined in Cooperstown.

The team itself would play just one more season in Brooklyn and then move west with the Giants to California in 1958, leaving the Yankees alone in New York. They'd pretty much had the place to themselves anyway.

Los Angeles Dodgers
1963-66

THE DODGERS IN LOS ANGELES WERE A PROFOUNDLY different team than the Dodgers in Brooklyn. The New Yorkers hit the ball, the Californians pitched it. And how! Consider what they did to the Yankees in the 1963 Series: Sandy Koufax, who was a cool 25–5 for the season, with 306 strikeouts in 311 innings and a 1.88 earned run average, shut them down 5–2 in the opener, setting a Series strikeout record, with 15. Johnny Podres won Game 2, 4–1, with relief help from bullpen ace Ron Perranoski, who was 16–3 with a 1.67 ERA in 69 appearances during the season. Don Drysdale, a 19-game winner, pitched a 1–0 shutout in Game 3, and then Koufax finished off the sweep with a 2–1 win in the final game. The Yankees, who had won six of seven Series from the Brooklyn Dodgers, scored a grand total of four runs in their first encounter with the Los Angeles Dodgers and set a four-game Series record for futility with their .171 team batting average.

There was more of the same in 1965 when the Dodgers beat the expansion Minnesota Twins, making their Series debut, in seven games. The Twins, with a lineup of sluggers that included Harmon Killebrew, Tony Oliva, Bob Allison and Zoilo Versalles, had been shut out only three times all season. The Dodgers blanked them that many times in the Series, and this after the Twins had actually beaten Hall of Famers Drysdale and Koufax in the first two games. Claude Osteen — acquired in a trade that sent the Dodgers' one very big home run hitter, the 6' 7", 250-pound Frank Howard, to Washington — won the third game 4–0; Drysdale won the fourth 7–2 and Koufax the fifth 7–0. Then after the Twins' Mudcat Grant, an aspiring nightclub singer, beat Osteen 5–1 in Game 6, Koufax came back to win the seventh 2–0.

Koufax, who refused to start the opener because of his observance of the Jewish holiday Yom Kippur, had an ERA in the Series of 0.38 with 29 strikeouts in 24 innings pitched. That was merely in keeping with the sort

of season he had experienced: 26–8, 2.04 with 27 complete games in 41 starts and a then major league record of 382 strikeouts in 335⅔ innings. He and Drysdale combined to win 49 games, 15 of them shutouts. The Dodgers had an anemic team batting average of .245 that season, and they hit a major league low 78 home runs. But with that pitching and shortstop Maury Wills stealing 94 bases, who needed hitters?

Well, as it turned out, they did the very next year when the Baltimore Orioles, making their World Series debut, swept them. Not that the Orioles, a hard-hitting team with Brooks and Frank Robinson and Boog Powell, overwhelmed them with their awesome power. In fact, the Baltimore team batting average of .200 was the lowest yet for any sweep winner and they scored a mere 13 runs in the four Series games. But when Sweet Lou Johnson crossed the plate in the third inning of Game 1, he scored the Dodgers' second and last run of the Series. The next three losses were all shutouts, pitched by Jim Palmer (6–0), Wally Bunker (1–0) and Dave McNally (1–0). The Dodgers set Series records for fewest runs scored (two), fewest hits (17), fewest total bases (23) and lowest batting average for a Series of any length (.142). They were scoreless in the final 33 innings of play.

They were also in for a jolt afterward when Koufax, who passed up a team junket to Japan, announced that, at age 30, he was retiring because of recurring arthritis in his pitching elbow. The Series aside, he went out a winner. He finished his farewell season with 27 wins and nine losses, 317 strikeouts in 323 innings and a league-leading 1.73 ERA. His record for the last four seasons was 97–27 with 1,228 strikeouts in 1,192⅔ innings pitched. But the glory was not enough to compensate for the pain in his left arm.

"I don't regret for one minute the 12 years I've spent in baseball," he said in his goodbye speech, "but I could regret one season too many."

St. Louis Cardinals
1964-68

THE CARDINALS, DORMANT FOR MUCH OF THE 50'S AND absent from the World Series since 1946, fluttered to life in the mid-60's with some of the old verve and panache. And pitching. In 1964 they slipped past the el foldo Phillies, who blew a 6½ game lead with 12 to play, and won the pennant on the last day of the season. So hopeless did the Cards' chances seem in midseason that owner Gussie Busch fired general manager Bing Devine in disgust. Manager Johnny Keane was so rankled by this premature sacking that, after beating the Yankees in seven games in the Series, he resigned and crossed over to become the new New York manager.

The '64 Cardinals got a booster shot in mid-June with the arrival of the exciting Lou Brock in a trade with the Cubs. Brock, who would eventually set major league records, since broken, for stolen bases in a season and a career, hit .348 in 103 games after the trade and stole 33 bases. He batted .300 in the Series and whacked a homer in the fifth inning of the final game as Bob Gibson struggled to a 7–5 victory.

Gibson fractured a leg when struck by a Roberto Clemente line drive in the '67 season, but he returned in time to pitch the win that clinched the pennant against Philadelphia in September. And he beat the Red Sox, winners in the American League after a thrilling four-team race, in the Series opener 2–1, striking out 10. The Sox took the second game behind Jim Lonborg's shutout pitching, and then, in the first Series game played in the Cardinals' new Busch Stadium, Nelson Briles pitched the home team to a 5–2 win. Gibson pitched a shutout in Game 4, but the Sox won the next two, setting up a Lonborg–Gibson confrontation in Game 7. It was no contest, Gibson winning his third game, 7–2. The glowering righthander had a Series ERA of 1.00 with 26 strikeouts in 27 innings.

It was the Cardinals' eighth win in 11 World Series and the first as general manager for Stan Musial, who retired as a player in 1963, and for Red Schoendienst,

who succeeded the defecting Keane as manager. The Cards were sparked in part that year by Ruth-buster Roger Maris, playing his first season in St. Louis, and by former Giant star Orlando Cepeda, playing his second. Behind the plate as ususal was the steady team leader, Tim McCarver. Dick Hughes, a nine-year minor leaguer, won 16 games for the Cardinals and, at 29, finished a close second to New York's Tom Seaver in the National League Rookie of the Year voting. Hughes, alas, would hurt his arm the following spring and win only two more games in the big leagues.

Gibson was as masterful in the 1968 Series as he had been in the previous two. But his team wasn't, losing in seven games to the Detroit Tigers and their plump lefthander, Mickey Lolich, who won three. In the opener Gibson was matched with 31-game winner Denny McLain, and again he was more than equal to the challenge, shutting out the Tigers 4–0 and establishing a World Series record by striking out 17. He won the fourth game 10–1, with a five-hitter, fanning 10 more and hitting his second World Series home run. It was his seventh straight complete game Series win, a record. In the sixth game the Bengals tied another record by scoring 10 times in the third inning in a 13–1 win over seven futile Cardinal pitchers. And then Lolich beat Gibson 4–1 in the finale, snapping the great righthander's victory string. It ended a surpassingly brilliant season on a sad note, for in '68, Gibson had won 22 games and lost nine, set a major league record (300 innings or more) with his 1.12 earned run average, completed 28 of 34 starts, led the league with 268 strikeouts, allowed just 198 hits in 304⅔ innings and pitched 13 shutouts, 10 of them between May and August, when he won 15 consecutive games. In his three outstanding World Series, he was 7–2, with 92 strikeouts in 81 innings.

In 1969 the rulemakers lowered the pitching mound five inches and lengthened the strike zone in hopes of putting a stop to this sort of thing.

Baltimore Orioles
1966-71

THESE BALTIMORE TEAMS SEEM-ingly had it all—pitching, hitting, defense—in abundance. But they also had an inexplicable penchant for being upset by lesser teams in the World Series, and that kept them from achieving true greatness. In the Orioles' first World Series, in 1966, though, they were the underdogs, and they astonished the experts by not only sweeping the Koufax-Drysdale Dodgers but shutting them out in the last three games. The two Dodger Hall of Fame pitchers would be little more than disgruntled bystanders as the youthful Oriole moundsmen—Jim Palmer, 20, Wally Bunker, 21, and Dave McNally, 23—methodically whitewashed them. The last Dodger run was scored in the third inning of Game 1 when McNally suffered control problems, walking three straight hitters. Moe Drabowsky relieved him and held the Dodgers at bay for the remaining 6⅔ innings, striking out 11, including a record six in a row. McNally recovered in time to win the fourth and final game 1–0.

The Orioles were ranked among baseball's elite by the time of their next Series appearance three years later under feisty Earl Weaver, managing his first full season after replacing Hank Bauer in July '68. They had won 109 games, finishing 19 ahead in the American League East, and then swept the Twins in the first year of league playoffs. And then they confounded their supporters by losing to the previously laughable New York Mets, four games to one, in the World Series.

They won 108 games the next year and again swept the Twins in the playoffs. Mike Cuellar (24–8), McNally (24–9) and Palmer (20–10) all won 20 or more. Third baseman Brooks Robinson, second baseman Davey Johnson and centerfielder Paul Blair won Gold Gloves. First baseman Boog Powell, who hit 35 homers and drove in 114 runs, was the league's Most Valuable Player. And eight players on the team hit home runs in double figures,

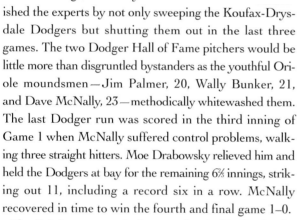

including Frank Robinson, with 25, and Brooks Robinson, with 18.

And this time they didn't disappoint in a World Series made memorable by the amazing defensive play of Brooks Robinson. In Game 1 the third baseman took a double away from Cincinnati's Lee May, throwing from his knees after tumbling into foul territory. He made two diving stops in Game 3 and in Game 5 soared once more into foul ground to spear Johnny Bench's line drive. And for good measure he hit .429 with two homers and six runs batted in. As a team the Orioles batted .292 with 10 homers and 33 runs scored in the five games. They won the first three, barely lost the fourth 6–5 and then won the finale 9–3 behind Cuellar.

This was a team that seemed invincible, the upset loss to the Mets dismissed by now as a meaningless anomaly. And when the Orioles won their third straight pennant, in '71, winning 100 or more games for the third straight time, and scored their third straight sweep in the playoffs, this time over the rising Oakland A's, they were rated overwhelming favorites to beat the apparently ragtag Pirates in the Series. The Robinsons and all the rest were back. Weaver was as smart and tenacious as ever. And this time they tied a major league record by having four pitchers—McNally (21–5), Pat Dobson (20–8), Palmer (20–9) and Cuellar (20–9)—win 20 or more. So how could they lose?

They did, dropping four of the last five Series games after winning the first two at home. The fourth game, won by the Pirates 4–3 at Pittsburgh, was significant for being the first, but regrettably not the last, World Series game played at night. The Pirates' Steve Blass beat Cuellar 2–1 in the seventh game, his second complete game victory in the Series. The two teams would meet again eight years later with remarkably similar results. But first they would have to wait for the passing of a couple of dynasties in, of all places, Oakland and Cincinnati.

'66 GEMS: DRABOWSKY (INSET LEFT) STRUCK OUT SIX IN A ROW IN GAME 1; PALMER WAS MASTERFUL IN GAME 2.

Oakland A's
1972-74

IT IS UNFORTUNATE INDEED THAT THE ONLY TEAM OTHER than the Yankee dreadnoughts of the 1930s and '50s to win three consecutive World Series should be recognized not so much for that considerable achievement as for off-field imbroglios and the eccentricities of an egomaniacal owner. But the Oakland A's of Sal Bando, Reggie Jackson, Joe Rudi, Bert Campaneris, Catfish Hunter, Vida Blue and Rollie Fingers are doomed, one fears, to go down in baseball history as Punch and Judy buffoons instead of as the consummate artists they were. Weren't they the guys who sported flourishing mustaches and wore those yellow-and-green softball uniforms? Weren't they always fighting among themselves? Didn't they have a mule for a mascot? And wasn't their owner, Charles O. Finley, something of an ass himself? Correct on all counts. But through it all, they could sure play baseball.

The A's were lightly regarded when they took on the up-and-coming Cincinnati Reds in the 1972 Series, but they won anyway in seven thrill-packed games, six of which were decided by one run. When they won a second pennant in '73 and beat the New York Mets in another seven-game Series, their and their proprietor's reputation for tomfoolery was pretty well entrenched. This was the Series in which Finley, fearful perhaps that his players were upstaging him, "fired" his second baseman, Mike Andrews, after that unfortunate made two costly errors in a wild second game during which the great Willie Mays, then 42, actually fell down chasing a fly ball. Andrews' teammates and the Oakland fans were outraged by this insensitive act, and baseball commissioner Bowie Kuhn immediately ordered Andrews reinstated. The cashiered second baseman eventually sued Finley for libel and slander.

Second base was something of an obsession with Charlie O. In '72 he tried rotating players at the position in almost every inning, and in '74 he experimented with seven men there before settling, as he always did, on the brilliant fielder Dick Green. Another obsession was the so-called "designated runner," a base-stealing specialist—first Allan (the Panamanian Express) Lewis, then trackman Herb Washington—with no other perceivable baseball talent. Lewis's and Washington's statistics in the *Encyclopedia of Baseball* make for interesting reading—more stolen bases and runs scored than times at bat.

Dick Williams, a conventional baseball man, wearied of these shenanigans after the team's second World Series triumph and resigned. To replace him, Charlie hired Alvin Dark, who had managed the Giants to the 1962 National League pennant but had lately become more Bible-thumping evangelist than baseball man. Dark nonetheless took the A's to their third consecutive pennant despite a bewildering succession of clubhouse altercations, one of which, between pitchers Fingers and John (Blue Moon) Odom, erupted the day before the start of the World Series with the Dodgers. Fingers required five stitches to close a nasty cut on the back of his head afterward. "I believe the record is 15 stitches," he remarked, "held by many." In what would for any other team be yet another disconcerting occurrence, 25-game winner Hunter announced before the Series that because Finley owed him back pay, he was declaring himself a free agent at the start of the next season. He did exactly that, was upheld by an arbitrator, and signed a $3 million contract with the Yankees.

Distractions aside, the A's whipped the Dodgers in five games in the first World Series played entirely in the state of California. The winning run in the final game came in the bottom of the seventh inning after play was halted for six minutes so that debris tossed onto the field by rowdy patrons could be removed. Rudi observed during this break that Dodger pitcher Mike Marshall had not continued to warm up, so he calculated that Marshall's first pitch would most likely be a simple fastball. It was, and Rudi hit it directly over the leftfield fence into those same roistering fans.

It was a play typical of a team that won not so much on brute force, even with Reggie Jackson, as on technical excellence. Too bad, it has never gotten its proper due.

FINLEY AND HIS BOISTEROUS A'S (CLOCKWISE FROM UPPER LEFT): FINGERS, RUDI, BLUE, GENE TENACE, CAMPANERIS, HUNTER, BANDO AND JACKSON.

Cincinnati Reds
1972-76

ANY DISCUSSION OF BASEBALL'S BEST TEAMS MUST NEC-
essarily include the so-called Big Red Machine operated by silver-thatched George (Sparky) Anderson. The
parts weren't all there yet, but Anderson won a pennant
in 1970, his first year at the controls, and another in '72,
when just a little tinkering was all that was needed. He
was beaten in the Series both years, then after winning
the National League West in '73 but losing to the Mets
in the playoffs and finishing second to the Dodgers in '74,
the Machine was properly tooled and ready to roll
through baseball as few teams have this side of the '27
Yankees.

The 1975 Reds won the West by 20 games, swept
the Pirates in the playoffs and won that memorable
Series with the Red Sox. The first five hitters in the batting order — Pete Rose, Joe Morgan, Johnny Bench,
Tony Perez and George Foster — were as formidable in
the variety of their skills as any in history. Rose led the
league in runs scored (112) and doubles (47) while
hitting .317. Morgan, the league's Most Valuable Player, hit .327, stole 67 bases and drove in 94 runs. Bench
hit 28 homers and drove in 110 runs. Perez hit 20 home
runs and drove in 109. Foster hit 23 homers. The only
missing ingredient appeared to be pitching, but then
Anderson, a.k.a. Captain Hook, approached this side of
the game from an unconventional viewpoint. The Reds'
mostly nondescript starters completed only 22 games all
season. But with help from a bullpen that led the league
with 50 saves, including 22 from Rawly Eastwick, three
of the pitchers — Jack Billingham, Don Gullett and
Gary Nolan — won 15 games apiece. The Reds may
have lacked a Mathewson, a Dean, a Grove or a Catfish
Hunter, but they did have a lot of busy arms. It was
pitching by committee.

In '76 the Machine ran even more smoothly. The
Reds won their division by 10 games and then took seven
straight postseason contests, sweeping the Phillies in the
league playoffs and the Yankees in the Series. They

became the first National League team since the 1921–22 New York Giants to win consecutive world championships. Rose, Morgan, Foster, rightfielder Ken Griffey and centerfielder Cesar Geronimo all hit above the .300 mark. Morgan won a second Most Valuable Player trophy, hitting .320 with 27 homers, 111 runs batted in and 60 stolen bases. Rose hit .323 and led the league in runs scored (130), hits (215) and doubles (42). Foster hit 29 home runs and led the league with 121 runs batted in. And Griffey had an amazing 37 infield hits, playing most of his games on artificial turf. In the four-game sweep of the once mighty Yankees, Bench hit a resounding .533 with two homers, a double, a triple and six RBIs.

Advised that Bench's counterpart, Thurman Munson, had hit .529 himself in the abbreviated Series, Anderson lectured World Series reporters against comparing anyone with Johnny Bench, the greatest catcher, in his opinion, who ever drew breath. A fuming Munson was sitting not 10 feet away in the post-Series interview room when Sparky delivered this paean. But, in truth, Bench, already in the Hall of Fame, was incomparable in his prime. And so was Morgan, also in the Hall. And Rose, not in the Hall.

Sparky himself may yet have a plaque in Cooperstown, what with his subsequent success, a 1984 World Series title, with a very good team in Detroit. But the Machine remains his favorite vehicle, and few managers ever enjoyed running a team more than this affable master of the malapropism and double negative. "This is show business," he once said. "I love writers. I love microphones. I love to be on television." This, of course, was Sparky Anderson talking, the public man. George Anderson is quite a different breed of cat, he will tell you, a quiet homebody content to stay clear of the public eye.

But when that Machine was on the move, Sparky-George was on a joyride to baseball immortality.

Oakland A's
1988-92

JUST WHEN IT LOOKED AS IF CHARLIE FINLEY HAD SUC-
cessfully killed off the franchise, saviors in blue jeans
arrived in the nick of time. The A's, their stars of the early
'70's either sold off or traded away, hit a nadir in 1979
when they lost 108 games and drew only 306,763 in total
home attendance. Then, in August 1980, the Haas family of Levi Strauss renown, bought the team from the
penurious Charlie O and started a long climb back to
respectability.

The new owners' first significant move was to hire
Tony La Russa, a smart, intense tactician, as manager mid-
way through the 1986 season. Then, by pumping money
into an all but abandoned farm system, they produced
three straight Rookies of the Year—outfielder Jose
Canseco in 1986, first baseman Mark McGwire in '87 and
shortstop Wally Weiss in '88. They also plucked Dave
Stewart, a supposedly washed-up pitcher, and Dave
Henderson, a peripatetic outfielder, from the free-agent
market. Stewart promptly won 20 or more games for four
consecutive years, 1987 through '90, and Henderson
had the best years of his career as an Athletic. In '87 they
acquired Dennis Eckersley in a trade with the Cubs
and, in a stroke of pure genius, persuaded him to switch
from starting to relieving. And then in 1989 they nego-
tiated the return of Oakland native Rickey Henderson
in a trade with the Yankees. The result was success
rivaling but not quite equaling that of the Mustache
Gang of the previous decade.

The Athletics won the first of three straight pennants
in '88, sweeping the Red Sox in the playoffs. And they
seemed well on their way to an opening game win over
the Dodgers in the World Series when disaster struck.
The A's, thanks to a Canseco grand slam homer, were
ahead 4–3 with two outs and nobody on base in the bottom of the ninth with Eckersley, who had a league-
leading 45 saves that year, on the mound to close out the
win. But Eckersley unaccountably walked Dodger
Mike Davis on four pitches, only his 13th walk of the

A TRIO OF SELF-STYLED OAKLAND OUTLAWS (FROM LEFT): CANSECO, HENDERSON AND McGWIRE.

entire season. And then with the count 3 and 2 on the next hitter, Kirk Gibson, who was so hobbled he could barely stand, let alone run, Eckersley threw a slider out over the plate. Gibson hit it into the rightfield pavilion at Dodger Stadium and painfully circled the bases with the winning run as the crowd went wild. "That home run was good for baseball," Eckersley said afterward, "but not for me." Or for his team. The A's never recovered from the shock and were beaten in five games, batting a woeful .177 in the process.

Only an earthquake could stop them—and then not for long—the next year. Overcoming a succession of injuries, including one to Canseco's wrist that caused him to miss 88 games, the A's won the West by seven games and knocked off Toronto in the playoffs. They won the first two games of the World Series in Oakland against the trans-Bay-rival Giants and were preparing to take the field for the start of Game 3 on October 17 when, shortly after 5 p.m., a quake measuring 7.1 shook Candlestick Park and rocked the entire Bay Area, causing extensive damage to freeways and bridges and to San Francisco's Marina neighborhood. The A's, shaken but unbowed when the Series finally resumed 10 days later, quickly finished off the Giants, 13–7 and 9–6, for a clean sweep.

In 1990, with Bob Welch winning 27 games and Stewart 22, the Athletics won a third pennant, again sweeping the beleagured Red Sox in the playoffs. But they were swept in turn by a hustling Cincinnati team that caught them unawares in the Series. The A's slipped all the way to fourth in the American League West the following year but revived to win the division in '92, only to lose to the eventual world-champion Toronto Blue Jays in the playoffs.

But four division titles, three American League championships and one World Series victory is not bad for a team that only a decade earlier looked to be slouching toward oblivion.

Players

Frank (Home Run) Baker

IN THE HEYDAY OF NICKNAMES, WHEN JUST ABOUT everyone on a ball field was a Hoss, a Rube, a Bugs, a Peach, a Rabbit, a Big Train or a Big Six, there was no moniker so evocative as the one they gave John Franklin Baker of Trappe, Maryland. And, considering the times, none more deserving. It's not easy living up to a name like Home Run Baker, particularly if, at 173 pounds, you are not physically imposing and if you've never hit more than 12 dingers in a season. But this was the Dead Ball era, and Baker's sobriquet was not awarded for any prolonged show of power. He hit no tape measure shots. There were no markers or plaques in the far reaches of those ancient ball yards to indicate where the mighty Baker had hit one. No, he earned the name for what he did in two days of the 1911 World Series. And the damn thing just stuck.

In Game 2 of that Series he hit a two-run homer off Rube Marquard in the sixth inning that beat the Giants 3–1 in Philadelphia. And then in Game 3 the next day in New York, he hit a ninth-inning solo homer off Christy Mathewson that tied the score of a game the Athletics eventually won 3–2 in the 11th. Actually, Baker was a superior hitter in just about every one of those World Series with the championship Athletics of 1910 to '14. He hit .409 in the 1910 defeat of the Chicago Cubs, .375 in the Series that gave him his name and .450 (with another home run) in the five-game defeat of the Giants in 1913. He dropped to .250 in 1914 when the A's fell in four to the Miracle Braves and Connie Mack decided to break up the ball club.

Mack was so short of cash then that he peddled off all of the $100,000 Infield except Baker, who decided to sit out the 1915 season rather than play in reduced circumstances. Mack then sold him to the Yankees in 1916, and in New York he was, in every sense, the biggest name on the team until the arrival in 1920 of a certain pitcher-outfielder from Boston. Baker, who had led the American League in homers for four straight years, 1911 through '14, hit 10 for the Yanks in 1916, second in the league only to teammate Wally Pipp's 12. Baker sat out the 1920 season mourning the death of his wife, so he missed the New York debut of Babe Ruth. Just as well. Ruth hit 54 homers that year, 25 more than his record 29 of the year before. The game had changed forever during Home Run Baker's sabbatical. It had also passed him by, causing the once proud nickname to seem merely comical.

Baker did appear in two Series for the Yankees. In 1921 he hit into an unusual double play to finish off the Giants' win over his team. With one out and Aaron Ward on first base, Baker hit a hard line drive toward rightfield. But Giant second baseman Johnny Rawlings was able to knock the ball down and throw to first in time to catch Home Run. Ward kept running, however, and first baseman George Kelly threw to third in time for Frankie Frisch to make the tag for the final out of the Series, the 4-3-5 double play giving the Giants a five games to three victory. The Giants swept the Yanks in 1922 and Baker appeared only once, as a pinch hitter.

He concluded his 13-year career after that Series, retiring with a .307 lifetime average and 96 home runs. Lost in all the hullabaloo over his Series heroics was the fact that Baker was an excellent fielder, one the Giants tried unsuccessfully to intimidate in that 1911 matchup. Twice in that Series, Giant centerfielder Fred Snodgrass slid spikes-high into third base, ripping Baker's uniform pants to shreds both times. Wrapped in a blanket to preserve his modesty, Home Run retreated to the dugout after each denuding and returned, newly trousered, to the fray. He was elected to the Hall of Fame in 1955.

Eddie Collins

THE PREMIER SECOND BASEMAN OF HIS ERA, EDDIE Collins was nevertheless exposed to some of the more bizarre, ugly and sublime events in World Series history. As the keystone of Connie Mack's legendary $100,000 Infield, Collins played in four Series with the Athletics and two more with the Chicago White Sox; one of these Series he would spend a lifetime trying to forget. In 34 Series games he hit for an average of .328, and his total of 14 stolen bases would be a record for 49 years until Lou Brock tied it in 1968. A native New Yorker, Collins joined the Athletics in 1906 directly from the Columbia University campus, and he would stay in the big leagues for 25 years, finishing with a lifetime batting average of .333. He had 3,311 hits, 1,818 runs scored and 743 stolen bases. Twice within 10 days in 1912, he stole six bases in a game. He led American League second basemen in fielding nine times, and no pivotman in big league history accepted more chances than his 14,156.

Collins hit .429 in the A's five-game win over the Cubs in the 1910 Series, stealing four bases. He slipped to .286 in the 1911 Series win over the Giants and then hit .421 with two triples and three steals in the 1913 triumph over those same Giants. His last Series with the A's was in 1914, when the Miracle Braves swept them in a stunning upset. Mack sold off his biggest stars after the disappointment, Collins going to the up-and-coming White Sox, who that year also acquired from Cleveland the superb hitter Shoeless Joe Jackson. The Sox were building, and in 1917 they won the pennant and then defeated John McGraw's Giants in the Series, four games to two. Collins hit .409 and Urban (Red) Faber won three games for Chicago.

It was in this Series that Collins was involved in one of the more ludicrous and, for McGraw, infuriating plays in Series history. The Sox were leading in games, three to two, as the Series moved to the Polo Grounds for Game 6. Faber and the Giants' Rube Benton were knotted in a scoreless pitching duel after three innings. Then in the fourth Collins hit a ground ball to third that Heinie Zimmerman—"the Great Zim," as he preferred to call himself—threw past first baseman Walter Holke for an error. Collins ended up on second. Jackson then lofted a fly ball to rightfield that Dave Robertson dropped for another error and Collins moved to third. He was off for home when Happy Felsch tapped a slow roller back to Benton, who threw to Zimmerman at third in an attempt to catch Collins in a rundown. Catcher Bill Rariden moved in to trap the runner, but the speedy Collins darted past him, leaving Zimmerman with nowhere to throw the ball. In an impossible situation, the plodding third baseman helplessly chased Collins across the plate as an amused umpire Bill Klem called the runner safe. It was the start of a game-and-Series-winning three-run rally for Chicago.

When he was accused later of committing a "boner," the Great Zim angrily replied, "Who the hell was I going to throw the ball to? Klem?"

The Sox slipped to sixth in 1918, but in 1919 came back with what should have been their strongest team under new manager William (Kid) Gleason, whose first act was to appoint Collins captain. Eddie was not popular, however, with one element on the team, and the Sox were soon divided into angry cliques, the straight arrows rallying behind Collins; the roughnecks, including Shoeless Joe, behind the unsavory first baseman, Chick Gandil. The Gandil group of eight soon became the infamous Black Sox who took money to fix the 1919 Series against Cincinnati. Collins and the rest of the "Clean Sox" played to win, but were unable to stave off the scandalous defeat. It would be the last World Series of Eddie Collins's impeccable career.

Bill Wambsganss

The Naps bought a shortstop named Wambsganss
Who is slated to fill Ray Chapman's pants.
But when he saw Ray
And the way he could play,
He muttered, "I haven't a clam's chance."

— Ring Lardner

WHEN A CLEVELAND SCOUT WHO HAD BEEN WATCHING Bill Wambsganss play shortstop for Cedar Rapids of the Central Association was asked by the front office, "What's he got?" he smartly replied, "Well, he has the funniest damn name I ever heard." And until the extraordinary events of October 10, 1920, just about the only thing famous about Bill Wambsganss *was* his funny name. Told once that Wambsganss was German for a kind of overcoat, Bill quickly picked up on the theme: "I don't know if it fits me or not, but I have worn it all my life and will probably carry it with me to the end. Anyway, it's a name people don't confuse with Miller or Jones."

Wambsganss was the son of a Lutheran clergyman from Indiana, and he himself spent two years at the St. Louis Theological Seminary before abandoning the cloth for baseball flannels. A slick fielder, he was called up late in the 1914 season as a shortstop, but he soon realized he had no chance of displacing the incumbent, Ray Chapman, so he gratefully shifted to second base, working so smoothly with Chapman that the Cleveland star once told him, "Bill, you're the only second baseman I'll ever play next to." The words were sadly prophetic.

A .278 hitter in 1919, Wambsganss slumped to .244 in the star-crossed championship season of 1920. But he had much else to be unhappy about that year, for on August 17, his close friend Chapman died after being hit in the temple by a pitch thrown by Yankee submarine-baller Carl Mays, the only big league player ever killed by a thrown ball. The second baseman was so despondent on the morning before the fifth game of the World Series with Brooklyn that year that he poured his heart out to another friend, F.C. Lane, the editor of *Baseball Magazine*. He had not yet recovered from Chapman's death, Wambsganss told Lane, and he feared he was hurting the team with his .154 Series batting average and poor fielding. Lane had never seen the quiet but usually cheerful Wamby so far down. "Stay with it, Bill," he said helplessly. "This could be your day."

It certainly was. The Series had been tied at that point, but in this fifth game at Cleveland's League Park, the Indians had moved out to a commanding 7–0 lead by the fifth inning. Pete Kilduff led off the Brooklyn half of the fifth with a single, and Otto Miller followed with another hit. With runners on first and second and nobody out, Wamby decided to play deep against the next batter, Clarence Mitchell, a good hitter for a pitcher, in hopes of cutting off anything up the middle. The count was 1 and 1 when Mitchell hit a hard line drive over second base, seemingly a sure hit. But Wamby made a leaping catch of the ball, managed to stay on his feet, then hurried to tag second base with Kilduff halfway to third. He turned to see Miller only a few feet away. "Tag him! Tag him!" bellowed Joe Sewell, Chapman's young replacement at short. And as Miller stood there stunned into inaction, Wamby did just that. Umpire Hank O'Day signaled the third out.

The crowd of 26,884 did not immediately react as Wambsganss jogged to the home dugout. Then there was an explosion of cheering, backslapping and straw-boater-flinging. The celebration lasted several minutes. Bill Wambsganss had at last made a name for himself. Or as Lardner wrote, "It was the first time in World Serious history that a man named Wambsganss had ever made a triple play assisted by consonants only."

Frankie Frisch

THE FORDHAM FLASH HAD ALREADY STARRED IN FOUR straight World Series—1921 through '24—for the New York Giants and was recognized as one of the game's premier second basemen when he and John McGraw clashed late in the 1926 season. Frisch had come to the Giants fresh from the Fordham University campus in 1919 and hit .363 in his four Series. He was the team captain in '26, but for the first time in 11 seasons, the Giants were buried in the second division (they would finish fifth), and McGraw's incessant carping so irritated the fiery infielder that he left the team during a midseason series in St. Louis and took the train back to New York by himself. Until then he had been considered the logical successor to McGraw as manager. After that he was finished in New York. That winter McGraw traded him to the Cardinals in a blockbuster deal that brought Rogers Hornsby to the Giants.

The trade was not exactly welcomed in St. Louis. Hornsby had just managed the Cardinals to their first World Series title and was still deemed the best righthanded hitter in the game. The St. Louis Chamber of Commerce passed a resolution denouncing the trade. Members of the Cardinals' board of directors threatened to resign. Various civic organizations vowed to boycott Cardinal games. And team owner Sam Breadon started receiving ominous letters. When Frisch committed two errors in a preseason exhibition game with the Browns, chants of "We want Hornsby" resounded off the walls of Sportsman's Park. But the Flash silenced that testy throng by hitting a game-winning homer in the eighth inning.

By the end of his first season there, Frisch was hearing nothing but hosannas from his former detractors. He hit .337 in 1927, had 52 extra-base hits and stole a league-leading 48 bases. "He saved my life," said Breadon. "If he hadn't come through like that, I'd have been finished. Cooked. I'd have had to leave town." The always truculent Hornsby, meanwhile, lasted only one season with McGraw. He hit .361, but Little Napoleon, chafing under the star's arrogance, sent him packing to the Boston Braves for 1928.

Frisch played in two losing Series with the Cards, in 1928 and '30, and a winner in '31, a year he was voted the league's MVP. Then early in the 1933 season he was tapped by Breadon and general manager Branch Rickey to replace Gabby Street as manager, even though he protested, rather feebly, that he was not yet ready to run a ball club. In a thrilling race with the Giants, he won the '34 pennant and beat the Tigers in the Series with his now legendary Gashouse Gang. At 36, Frisch didn't have a bad year himself, hitting .305, driving in 75 runs and scoring 74. And he could still give speedsters like Pepper Martin and Ernie Orsatti a run for their money. In fact, three years earlier he had beaten the two outfielders in a match race from foul line to foul line.

Frisch was an unusual if apparently ideal choice to manage the playful Gashousers, for though he talked and played tough, he was actually a cultivated man who enjoyed good books, the theater and travel abroad. The constant practical joking of his players drove him nearly to distraction, but winning, he found, was the perfect antidote. The gang didn't last long, though, and Frisch didn't survive much longer. He benched himself as a player after a game early in 1937 when the young centerfielder, Terry Moore, nearly passed him on the base paths. "Any time they can run down the Flash," he commented sadly, "it's time to quit." And he didn't make it through the 1938 season as manager before Breadon and Rickey sacked him.

Frisch finished up his managerial career in Pittsburgh and with the Cubs before finally retiring in 1951. He was elected to the Hall of Fame in 1947.

Babe Ruth

"HE WAS UNIQUE," SAID HIS OLD TEAMMATE JUMPIN'
Joe Dugan. "There was nobody like him. He was …
a god." In truth, as the years pass, Babe Ruth does not
seem so much mortal as part of our native mythology,
a figure from legend like Paul Bunyan or John Henry.
He was the Bambino, the Sultan of Swat, who lived life
on the grand scale, satisfying gargantuan appetites
for food, hooch, women and money, all the while hitting those unforgettable homers and generally playing
baseball the way no one ever has. In the end, of
course, he was regrettably all too human.

Many of the Babe's supposedly unbeatable records
have been beaten. Roger Maris topped his 60 homers
in a season in 1961. Hank Aaron passed his 714 career
homers in 1974. Whitey Ford bettered his pitching
record of 29⅔ scoreless World Series innings in the 1961
Series. Mickey Mantle surpassed his World Series
innings in the 1964 Series. And Billy Hatcher, who hit
.750 for Cincinnati in the four-game 1990 Series, beat
his record World Series average of .625.

But Ruth still has enough records to fill volumes. He
led the American League in home runs 12 times. He hit
more than 40 homers in a season 11 times and more
than 50 two years in a row twice. He hit two homers
in a game 71 times. His average of one home run for
every 11.8 times at bat has never been approached. He
had the three highest slugging averages in history—.847
in 1920, .846 in '21 and .772 in '27. His *career* slugging
average is .690, a figure so high that only four players
have surpassed it in a single season in 65 years. In 1920
and '27 Ruth hit more homers than any *team* in the
American League. The 60-homer season aside, consider
the years he had in 1920 and '21. In '20 he hit .376 with
54 homers, 36 doubles and nine triples. He scored 158
runs and batted in 137. In 1921 he had 457 total
bases, 119 extra-base hits—59 homers, 16 triples and

44 doubles—and averaged .378. He drove in 171 runs
and scored 177. Then in 1923 he hit .393 (with 41
homers), the highest batting average in Yankee history.
His lifetime average was .342.

In 10 World Series the Babe averaged .326 with 15
homers, 37 runs scored and 33 RBIs. Twice he hit three
homers in a single Series game. His .625 average in 1928
was tops for 62 years. And this is not to mention the
famous "called shot" of 1932, which mythologists consider his crowning moment. Ruth even set records
for suspensions in a season (five in 1922) and for the
highest fine ($5,000 in 1925 for insubordination). His
$80,000 salary in 1930 was the highest by far up to then
and was not exceeded until after World War II. When
it was pointed out to him that he was being paid more
than President Hoover, the Babe tartly responded,
"I had a better year than he did."

But his last year was not so good. He left the Yankees
in 1935 to play for and supposedly become a vice-
president of the Boston Braves. The front office deal
never materialized, and he played only 28 games that
year before retiring for keeps. Early in that season,
though, he hit three homers in one game against Pittsburgh. The last of these, the 714th and last of his
career, cleared the roof over the double-decked rightfield stands in Forbes Field and was estimated to
have traveled more than 600 feet, the longest homer
ever hit in that ballpark. How else could he have finished off a career?

Ruth had long aspired to manage a major league
team, but he never got the opportunity, his own reputation for recklessness damaging his chances. He
tried coaching with the Brooklyn Dodgers in 1938, but
that was it. Ten years later, at age 53, he died of throat
cancer. But Joe Dugan was right: There was nobody
like him. There never will be.

Goose Goslin

HE WAS "JUST A BIG OL' COUNTRY BOY" FROM SOUTH Jersey "havin' the time of my life." And "in those days," he told Lawrence Ritter in *The Glory of Their Times*, "I'd go out and fight a bull without a sword and never know the difference. … I'd have paid them to let me play." He didn't have to do that, but the Goose was certainly a money ballplayer. And he had a fantastic knack for being in the right place at the right time.

In 1924 he batted .344, hit three homers, drove in seven runs and established a then World Series record with six straight hits, in Games 3, 4 and 5, as the Washington Senators won their first world championship. Eleven years later he drove in the winning run with two outs in the ninth inning of the final game to give the Detroit Tigers their first World Series title. Championship teams just seemed to find him. He played in the Senators' first two Series, then early in the 1930 season he was traded to the St. Louis Browns. The Senators stayed away from postseason play until they got him back in 1933 and then lost to the Giants in the Series, four games to one. Washington owner Clark Griffith told Goose after the Series that, with the Great Depression, he could no longer afford him, so he was selling him to Detroit. The Tigers hadn't been in a Series since 1909, but with Goose in the lineup, they made it in 1934 and '35. The man was a lucky charm.

He was also an exceptional ballplayer. In the Senators' championship season of 1924, he hit .344 and led the American League in runs batted in with 129. In 1928 he won the batting championship by a single percentage point on the last day of the season over Heinie Manush of the St. Louis Browns. To add to the drama, the Senators and the Browns were playing each other that day. Goslin was ahead in the batting race approaching his final time at bat, so manager Bucky Harris gave him the option of sitting down for a pinch hitter. The

Goose was fully prepared to accept that generous offer until teammate Joe Judge told him that leaving the game would make him look "yellow." Goslin decided to take his cuts. But umpire Bill Guthrie called two quick strikes on him, and when Goslin, seeing the batting title go down the drain, protested vigorously, Guthrie told him that no matter what vile things he said, he was not going to be tossed out of the game. Goslin stepped back in and got the hit that clinched the title. It was, he protested, "a lucky hit."

He got lucky again, he insisted, in the ninth inning of the sixth game of the 1935 Series with the Cubs. With one out and the score tied 3–3, Detroit's catcher-manager Mickey Cochrane singled off Chicago starter Larry French. Cochrane moved to second when Charlie Gehringer grounded out. Now, with two outs, the winning run on second and the Series on the line, Goslin came to bat. He turned to umpire Ernie Quigley and said, "If they pitch that ball over this plate, you can go take that monkey suit off." French's first pitch was over the plate, and Goslin ripped it to rightfield for the winner, as long-suffering Detroit fans launched a victory celebration that lasted into the next day.

Goslin finished his 18-year career where he started it, in Washington, D.C. The Tigers released him after the 1937 season, and Griffith, who couldn't afford him three years earlier, invited him to rejoin the Senators and "finish up." It was a reunion of sorts, since Harris, after managerial interludes in Detroit and Boston, was also back skippering the team. That season Goslin got the last nine of his 2,735 hits and the last eight of his 1,609 runs batted in. He knew he was finished when, swinging at a Lefty Grove fastball, he wrenched his back. Harris called him back to the dugout, and that, said Goslin, "was the only time a pinch hitter was ever put in for the ol' Goose."

Lou Gehrig

ON ANY OTHER TEAM AND IN ANY OTHER TIME, HENRY Louis Gehrig would have been considered a phenomenon. But his destiny, it seemed, was to be the workaday supporting player. Only in death would he get top billing. And yet, overshadowed as he was for much of his career, he remains today a true American icon.

The manner in which he broke into the Yankee lineup has even become an enduring folktale. On June 1, 1925, Gehrig was sent in as a pinch hitter for shortstop Pee Wee Wanninger, and though no one at the time knew it, this was to become a historic occasion. The next day the Yankees' regular first baseman, Wally Pipp, reported to the clubhouse complaining of a headache. Yankee manager Miller Huggins gave Pipp the day off, replacing him with the 21-year-old Gehrig, who in the previous two seasons had appeared in only 23 games, coming to bat a total of 38 times. Gehrig got three hits that day against Washington and was in the lineup to stay for the next 14 years, playing in a record 2,130 consecutive games from the day he hit for Wanninger. Pipp, traded the next year to Cincinnati, has since become a verb in the baseball vernacular, as in, "He called in sick and got Wally Pipped."

Gehrig hit .295 in 1925. He would not hit below .300 again until his final complete season, 1938. For 13 straight years he would score and drive in 100 runs or more. In 1927, the year he and Babe Ruth hit 107 homers between them, he set an American League record for RBIs, with 175, but he would break that four years later by driving in 184. In 1930 and '31 he drove in the astonishing total of 358 runs, an average of 179. He hit more than 40 homers five times, including 49 twice. In 1934 he had 18 more homers than strikeouts. He won the Triple Crown that year, hitting .363 with 49 homers and 165 RBIs. He is the alltime leader in grand slam homers, with 23. And though not fast on

his feet, he had 15 steals of home. In seven World Series he hit .361 with 10 homers and 35 RBIs.

And yet his biggest moments were usually diminished by showier events. He hit a rousing .545 in the 1928 Series, but Ruth hit .625. He hit three homers in the 1932 World Series against the Cubs and batted .529 with eight RBIs in just four games, but all this was forgotten when Ruth walloped his "called shot" off Charlie Root in Game 3. Gehrig, naturally, followed that memorable clout with a homer of his own. On June 3, 1932, he hit four home runs in a single game, the first player to accomplish that feat in this century. But on that same day John McGraw captured the headlines by announcing his retirement after 31 years as manager of the New York Giants. The year he won the Triple Crown, Mickey Cochrane, who hit 43 percentage points lower, won the league's Most Valuable Player award. And then, in 1936, with Ruth retired, it looked as if for once Gehrig would have center stage all to himself, when along came a glamorous rookie from San Francisco named Joe DiMaggio to steal his thunder.

But Gehrig would yet win the hearts of Americans. On May 2, 1939, increasingly weak and strangely uncoordinated, he took himself out of the Yankee lineup, ending his longevity streak. A few weeks later it was learned he was suffering from amyotrophic lateral sclerosis, a paralyzing and invariably fatal disease. On July 4 of that year, on Lou Gehrig Day, before 61,808 fans at Yankee Stadium, he delivered his now famous farewell address: "Fans, for the past two weeks you have been reading about a bad break I got. Yet today I consider myself the luckiest man on the face of the earth…."

Lou Gehrig died on June 2, 1941, 16 years to the day after he replaced Wally Pipp. The disease that killed him now bears his name.

Al Simmons

A WISTFUL CONNIE MACK WOULD SAY OF HIS STAR leftfielder, "Oh, how I wish I had nine players named Al Simmons." The truth is, he didn't even have one, since the Milwaukee-born Simmons's real name was Aloys Szymanski. Nine players with that name would have wreaked havoc with the box scores of the day, but like many athletes of foreign origin in the '20s and '30s, Simmons had his name Americanized. So, for that matter, did Connie Mack, né Cornelius McGillicuddy.

For that matter, when Simmons first joined the Athletics' staff in 1925, his teammates quickly nicknamed him Bucketfoot Al, for his "foot-in-the-bucket" batting stance that had his left foot aimed somewhere between third base and the opposing team's dugout. Simmons always looked as if, at the first glimpse of a pitched ball, he would depart for the safety of the third base box seats. That was scarcely what he had in mind, though, for, exaggerated stance aside, he was one of the finest right-handed hitters the game has known. He hit a relatively modest .308 as a rookie, then soared to .384 his second year, amassing 253 hits, the second greatest number in American League history behind George Sisler's 257 in 1920. In 1927 his average climbed to .392. He was the league's Most Valuable Player when the A's won the pennant in 1929, hitting .365 with 34 homers and a league-leading 157 RBIs. And he hit an even .300 with two homers in his team's five-game World Series win over the Cubs that year. It was Simmons who launched the Athletics' famous 10-run seventh-inning rally in Game 4 with a leadoff homer. He also singled in a second at bat that inning and scored the ninth run. The Cubs were cooked after that.

For much of his career, opposing pitchers tried to pitch Bucketfoot Al outside, reasoning imperfectly that with that stance he could never reach a ball low and away. Wrong. Dead wrong. Simmons, who hit to all fields, simply slammed those outside pitches up the middle of the diamond with his exceptionally long bat. Charlie Gehringer, the Tigers' Hall of Fame second baseman, said Simmons hit some of the hardest grounders he ever fielded. "He could blister it," said Gehringer. "He hit a miserable ground ball."

In 1930 Simmons led the league with a .381 average, hit 36 homers, drove in 165 runs and scored 152. He hit .364 in the Athletics' six-game Series win over the Cardinals. In '31 he led the league again with a .390 average and then hit .333 in the Series loss to Pepper Martin and the Cards. In those three straight Series, Simmons hit .333 with 14 runs scored and 17 driven in. He hit two homers in each of them.

Those great Mack teams, like the earlier champions of 1910 to '14, were doomed by the franchise's financial difficulties to be torn asunder. But they were wondrous to behold while they were intact. Simmons, the cleanup hitter, was flanked by Mickey Cochrane, batting third, and by Jimmie Foxx. All three are in the Hall of Fame. But in the midst of the Great Depression, all three were sold to other clubs by their periodically impoverished employer: Simmons, along with Mule Haas and Jimmy Dykes, to the White Sox for $150,000 in 1933, Cochrane to Detroit for $100,000 in 1934 and Foxx to Boston for $150,000 in 1935. It would be 41 years before the Athletics would win another pennant, and by then the team would be in Oakland.

Al Simmons would enjoy a few more good seasons after Mack sold him—he hit .331 and .344 his first two years with Chicago—but the real glory years were behind him. World War II kept him active sporadically on talent-poor teams until his career ended, in 1944, where it began, with the Athletics. He finished with a lifetime average of .334. He had 2,927 hits, 307 homers and 1,827 runs batted in.

Pepper Martin

TO SAY, "THEY DON'T MAKE 'EM LIKE THAT ANYMORE," is to deprive Pepper Martin of his due, because they never made 'em like Pepper to begin with. Indeed, when we compare the young plutocrats playing today with this Wild Hoss of the Osage, we can see just how far civilization has advanced … or declined. The moderns may be richer, but no one ever had a better time playing baseball than this man-child from the Ozarks. Martin's career average for 13 big league seasons was .298. He led the league in stolen bases three times and in runs scored once. But he saved his best for the World Series, personally unhinging the Athletics by hitting .500 for the Cardinals in '31 and then returning three years later as the ringleader of the Gashouse Gang to beat the Tigers with a .355 average and eight runs scored. In the two Series, Martin belted a cumulative .418 with 14 runs scored and eight driven in.

Pepper may have been even more famous off the field. He was the conductor and star soloist (mouth organ) of the Gashousers' Mudcat Band and the instigator of the sleight-of-hand pepper games (no ball) that entertained fans at Sportsman's Park. His enthusiasm for midget auto racing was such that on road trips he often carried spare parts with him in a wardrobe trunk. Once he interrupted a serious team meeting by inquiring of manager Frankie Frisch, "Frank, I can't decide whether to paint my midget auto yellow or red. What do you think?" What Frisch thought could be heard in Hawaii. Frisch actually loved him, but there were times when Martin nearly drove him over the edge. Pepper was fond of dropping water bags out of hotel windows onto busy urban sidewalks, and when one of these landed at Frisch's feet, ruining a new suit, Martin promised to hit a game-winning home run as atonement. The next day, he did.

Pepper was notorious for arriving at spring training under unusual circumstances. En route to Florida one year he stopped at a small-town hotel. He'd done some hunting and was absentmindedly carrying his shotgun when he entered the lobby. When the clerk called his attention to this, Martin puckishly signed the register Pretty Boy Floyd. Heavily armed sheriff's deputies arrived moments later to capture the notorious gunman, and it was some time before Pepper could convince them he was simply a prankster, not a gangster.

Once, though, he actually was arrested on the way to training camp. Pepper preferred, particularly early in his underpaid career, to hop freights east from Oklahoma rather than pay train fare. One year he was rousted along with a boxcar of hobos in Thomasville, Georgia, and jailed for the night. He borrowed the five-dollar bail money from a local minister and then borrowed another dollar to buy cigarettes for his impoverished cell mates. Pepper arrived for spring training with a three-day growth of beard and wearing tattered and greasy overalls. He paid the minister back with his first paycheck.

He was a superstitious man who believed hairpins were talismans, so he pocketed them wherever he found them. As a joke on a joker, several St. Louis sportswriters spread hairpins all over the lobby of the team's road hotel one night while Pepper was out on the town. To their dismay, Joe (Ducky) Medwick arrived before Martin and inexplicably began picking up the pins. "Hey, those are for Martin," writer J. Roy Stockton protested. Medwick snapped back, "Let him find his own hairpins."

After an absence of three seasons, Martin, then 40, helped fill out the Cardinals' wartime roster in 1944, playing alongside a young Stan Musial, then about to enter the service. In one game Musial lost a fly ball in the sun, staggered under it, and it hit him directly on top of the head. Martin retrieved the carom and, after firing the ball back into the infield, inquired of Musial's health. "I'm O.K.," Stan the Man reassured him. "Then," said Martin, "you won't mind if I laugh." And he did, rolling on the turf and kicking his heels. The game had to be held up until this paroxysm subsided.

Baseball was always, above all else, a lot of fun for Pepper Martin.

Joe DiMaggio

THE YANKEE CLIPPER YET REMAINS, 46 YEARS AFTER HIS last game, the personification of athletic grace and perfection. The name DiMaggio is as familiar to most Americans as Lincoln or Washington. His enduring popularity is, in itself, a curious thing, since he has done little to perpetuate his image, preferring to lead an almost cloistered existence in these, his declining years.

But in his prime there was nothing he could not do on a baseball diamond and do better than anyone else. He hit for average and power. He ran the bases with speed and cunning. And he is yet considered by many experts to have been the finest centerfielder who ever played. But could he bunt? "I don't know," answered his longtime manager, Joe McCarthy, "nor have I any intention of ever finding out."

DiMaggio's best seasons were before World War II. He came to the Yankees as a trumpeted rookie in 1936 and almost immediately justified his advance billing by hitting .323, scoring 132 runs and driving in 125, while blasting 29 homers, 44 doubles and a league-leading 15 triples. In his sophomore year 1937, he led the American League in home runs with 46, an unusual feat for a righthanded batter playing in the old Yankee Stadium with its enormous power alley in leftfield. He led the league in hitting with a .381 average in 1939 and again in '40 with .352. And in 1941 he set a record that may never be broken by hitting in 56 consecutive games. He spent three years in the Army, all of them peak playing years, and was never really the same afterward as increasing injuries and age robbed him of his once consummate skills. Still, he won his third MVP award in 1947 and in '48 led the league in homers with 39 and in RBIs with 155. Unlike most power hitters, DiMaggio was also a contact hitter, and he almost never struck out. He never fanned more than 39 times in a season, and in '41, a year he batted .357 and hit 30 homers,

he struck out only 13 times in 541 times at bat. For his career, he very nearly had more homers than strikeouts—361 to 369. Compare that with, say, Reggie Jackson's career 563 homers and 2,597 strikeouts, and it is apparent just how remarkable that statistic is.

DiMaggio led the Yankees to victory in nine of 10 World Series. And it was he who started the winning rally in the fourth game of the 1941 Series after Tommy Henrich had apparently struck out to end the game. But Mickey Owen dropped the third strike, Henrich reached base safely, and DiMaggio singled to open the way for a four-run inning. DiMaggio retired after the 1951 Series, explaining that at 37 he could no longer measure up to his own high standards. It was, of course, a dignified exit.

As a young man DiMaggio was an enigma personally. Almost pathologically shy and reserved, he nevertheless enjoyed appearing in some of New York's most public night spots, including Toots Shor's and the Stork Club, and he liked the company of actors and comedians. He also married two actresses: Dorothy Arnold and, in a universally publicized union, Marilyn Monroe, who has since become a mythic figure herself. And yet he would never publicly discuss his very public private life.

For years he has defined that undefinable quality called class. At 82 he is a handsome man who dresses tastefully and carries himself well. He still knows instinctively when to keep his mouth shut. And he has an ingrained sense of loyalty that has kept him close, to this day, with many of his old friends from the San Francisco waterfront. He was a pallbearer at the funeral of his longtime friend, the tavern owner Reno Barsocchini, a few years ago. With these old chums he could always speak his mind. The rest of the time, he keeps quiet. Maybe that's class.

Yogi Berra

HIS REPUTATION AS A ... WELL ... PHRASEMAKER HAS, with time, obscured his brilliance as a ballplayer. And, in a way, that's a shame, although Yogi Berra may someday outquote Shakespeare in *Bartlett's* if the people who concoct malapropisms for him stay as busy as they have been over the past 45 years. Yogi didn't really need all that much help from ghostwriters, though, because the things he actually did say are quaint enough. When his Yankee roommate Bobby Brown had just finished ploughing through a medical textbook, Yogi really did ask him, "How'd it come out?" And he did advise a struggling hitter, seeking a role model in Frank Robinson, "If you can't imitate him, don't copy him." And he did say of the old Yankee Stadium outfield, "It gets late early there." And out of gratitude for a celebration in his honor, he did thank "all those who made this day necessary."

The rest you can look up. Lawrence Peter Berra got his nickname when some of his childhood buddies saw a resemblance between him and an Indian fakir they'd seen in a movie. He came up to the Yankees as a raw talent in 1946, as much an outfielder then as a catcher. At 5'7" and 190 pounds, he looked, said Yankee president Larry McPhail, "like the bottom man on an unemployed acrobatic team." And yet he was astonishingly agile. As an inexperienced catcher in 1947, he once fielded a bunt in a game against the St. Louis Browns and in two lightning motions, tagged the hitter and a runner coming home from third on a squeeze play. "I just tagged everything in sight," he explained, "including the umpire." When Casey Stengel took over as Yankee manager in 1949, he called a halt to any more position-shuffling and told Yogi to stay behind the plate. Coach Bill Dickey, a great catcher in his day, was assigned to Berra's education. "Bill," a studious Yogi said, "is learning me his experiences." He learned him well.

Between 1950 and '57, Yogi caught, in succession, 148, 141, 140, 133, 149, 145, 135 and 121 games. A bad-ball hitter, he nevertheless walloped 20 or more home runs for 10 straight years, 1949 through '58, and had four straight 100 or more RBI seasons, 1953 through '56. In his 19-year career (17 full seasons) he hit 358 home runs, 313 as a catcher. And he won the Most Valuable Player award in the American League three times.

Berra played in a record 14 World Series, 10 of which the Yankees won. He holds the record for most games played (75) and most hits (71), and with 39 RBIs he is one behind the record holder, his old teammate Mickey Mantle. He got off to a relatively slow start in Series play, with just 19 hits, four homers and eight RBIs in his first five. Then in 1953 he batted .429 and in Game 1 performed the remarkable feat of throwing out two Dodgers at third base on successive sacrifice attempts. He hit .417 in the 1955 Series loss to the Dodgers. In 1956 he hit a grand slam homer in Game 2, caught the only perfect game in Series history in Game 5 and hit two more homers in Game 7. He batted .360 for the Series, with 10 RBIs. He hit .320 in the 1957 Series and after slumping to .222 in 1958, hit .318 with eight RBIs in the 1960 Series. In seven World Series between 1953 and '61, he had 54 hits, including eight doubles and eight homers, and he drove in 31 runs.

Berra managed the Yankees to the 1964 pennant, then not only lost to the Cardinals in the Series but lost his job to the winning manager, Johnny Keane. He managed the Mets to the National League pennant in 1973, but lost again in the Series, this time to the boisterous Oakland A's.

But Yogi is still around, and as he may or may not have said, "It ain't over 'till it's over."

Duke Snider

BORN EDWIN DONALD SNIDER IN LOS ANGELES, HE became the Duke of Flatbush, one of three Hall of Fame centerfielders—"Willie, Mickey and the Duke"—playing in New York during the city's Golden Age of Baseball in the 1950s. Duke Snider was the first to arrive on the scene, as a 20-year-old in 1947. Two years later he would be a Dodger regular, hitting .292 with 23 homers and 100 runs scored and playing in the first of six World Series. Ebbets Field, with its 297-foot foul line and 344-foot power alley in rightfield, seemed tailored for the Duke's quick and powerful lefthanded batting stroke, and no Dodger ever took greater advantage of the park. He hit 40 or more homers for five straight years, from 1953 through '57. In 1955 he hit 40 and led the league with 136 RBIs and 126 runs scored. And in the '55 World Series, the first the Dodgers would win in seven tries, he hit four homers and drove in seven runs. Three years earlier he also hit four Series homers, and is still the only player in either league to hit that many homers in a Series twice. His 11 homers and 26 runs batted in are Series records for the National League.

The Duke had it all in Brooklyn. He hit for power and average—above .300 for four years in a row with highs of .341 in '54 and .336 in '53—and he was the eagle of the Dodger outfield. At the same time, he carried on a love-hate relationship with the sometimes querulous but always dead loyal Brooklyn fans. Once after being booed in 1955 he remarked testily, "Brooklyn fans are the worst in baseball. They don't deserve a pennant." They are words he probably would have preferred eating, since that year the Dodgers beat the Yankees for their first world championship and were celebrated as heroes for months afterward. The next year Snider and a fan actually came to blows after an exchange of insults outside the ballpark.

But like so many of the Boys of Summer, the Duke hated leaving Flatbush, even though when the team moved to Los Angeles in 1958, he was coming home. It turns out he had good reason for his reluctance to leave, for the team's temporary new home at the Los Angeles Coliseum had a power alley in rightfield of 440 feet. Righthanded batters had it considerably better, since it was only 250 feet down the line to the leftfield screen. As if that weren't daunting enough, Snider reinjured an already gimpy left knee in a spring training auto accident and later hurt his arm trying foolishly and unsuccessfully to throw a ball completely out of the towering Coliseum. He played in only 106 games his homecoming year and hit just 15 homers, only six in the Coliseum and none over that remote rightfield fence—this after hitting at least 23 the previous five years in Ebbets Field alone. The Dodgers finished seventh that year.

Both Snider and the team bounced back in '59, Duke hitting .308 with 23 homers and 88 RBIs in 126 games. The fence in right center was brought in to a much more accessible 375 feet, and Snider hit eight of his 13 homers in the Coliseum over it, the first on May 4. But at 33 the once proud Duke had grown prematurely old as a ballplayer. The knee never did heal completely, the arm was sore and the hair graying. His injuries limited his time to just four games and 10 at bats in the '59 Series win over the White Sox, but one of his two hits was a homer in the clinching seventh game. In the ninth inning of that same game, though, he was lifted for pinch-hitter Chuck Essegian, and he, too, homered.

It would be the Duke's last World Series. He was gone to the hapless Mets in '63 when the Dodgers blanked the Yankees in four that year. And he finished his career a year later, playing, for of all people, the Giants.

Whitey Ford

THIS SON OF A QUEENS SALOONKEEPER HOLDS VIR-tually every important World Series pitching record, including most wins (10) and most losses (eight). He appeared in 11 Series, and had it not been for Army duty in the Korean War, he would have been in two more, in 1951 and '52. He had the most Series starts (22) and the most opening game starts (eight). He pitched the most innings (146), had the most strike-outs (94) and the most walks (34). And he pitched 33⅔ consecutive scoreless innings, breaking the old record of 29⅔ set by Babe Ruth in his pre-Yankee years as a Red Sox pitcher. Whitey's regular-season winning percentage of .690 (236 wins, 106 losses) is also the highest for any 200-game winner in this century.

Ford's remarkable career started on July 17, 1950, when he was called up by the Yankees after four years in the minors. He instantly reeled off nine con-secutive wins and didn't lose until September 27 in relief against the Athletics. In the World Series that year he had a shutout working with two outs in the ninth inning of Game 4 against the Phillies when Gene Woodling dropped a fly ball, allowing two runs to score. Ford then gave up a single and manager Casey Stengel lifted the rookie for the veteran Allie Reynolds, who got the final out of the Series.

Ford rejoined the Yanks in 1953 after his Army hitch and scarcely skipped a beat, winning 18 games in Stengel's fifth straight championship year. His streak of scoreless innings started in the 1960 Series when he blanked the Pirates in his only two starts. Stengel, in fact, was widely criticized that year for not using Whitey in the opener so that he might have had three shots at the ultimately victorious Pirates. But Casey had always exercised caution with Ford, start-ing him no more than 33 times in a season. Ralph Houk, who succeeded Stengel in 1961, exercised no such restraint, calling on him 39 times his first year and 37 each of the next two seasons. Ford responded to the heavier work load with 25–4, 17–8 and 24–7 seasons.

At a stocky 5' 10" and 178 pounds, he was never an overpowering pitcher, but he did have a sneaky fastball to go with one of the best curveballs in the game and an assortment of trick pitches, not all of which conformed to the rules. Ford got more pleasure out of deceiving hit-ters than blowing the ball by them, and his deceptions involved use not only of the conventional spitter but of a pitch pretty much of his own invention, the "mudball," which was one part saliva and one part dirt from the mound. He did not, however, throw these disreputable pitches as often as the hitters expected him to, thus adding to the confusion upon which he thrived.

Mostly Ford had uncommon poise and confidence. "I have never seen pressure bother him," said Stengel pitch-ing coach Jim Turner, "and the Yankees during those days were always under pressure." Watching Ford, said fellow Yankee pitcher Ralph Terry, "was like watching a pitching textbook in the flesh."

Ford was a cocky figure on the mound, but off it he was, according to teammate Tony Kubek, "shocking-ly humble." He was, with Mickey Mantle and Billy Mar-tin, part of the nightlife brigade—"the Irish guy who laughs all the time," said Kubek—and an inveterate prac-tical joker. But he could be surprisingly sensitive. "I loved playing behind Whitey," said first baseman Moose Skowron, "because he never got on me if I made an error." And catcher Johnny Blanchard recalls an occa-sion when Ford summoned him from behind the plate. "What's wrong?" asked Blanchard. "Nothing," replied Whitey. "Then why bring me out here?" "Because," said Ford, "I figured you could use the break."

"Name another pitcher who ever said something like that to a catcher," said Blanchard in wonderment.

Mickey Mantle

THOSE MELANCHOLY WORDS "IF ONLY" APPLY ALL TOO well to the brilliant and yet unfulfilled career of Mickey Mantle, as in, "if only he could have stayed healthy." But the Mick grew up with the specter of death in the family, and he halfway expected the Reaper to appear at any minute on his doorstep. Both his father and his grandfather, victims of Hodgkin's disease, died before they reached 45, and Mickey, operating under the assumption that he too would have a short life, lived every minute as if it were his last. His death in 1995 at the age of 63 was ample proof of his less than careful lifestyle. And yet, with all of the injuries he suffered and all the late hours he routinely kept, he had a Hall of Fame career equaled by few.

Mantle got into his first World Series as a rookie in 1951, but he didn't last long, spraining his right knee after stepping on a drain cover in the Yankee Stadium outfield. Mantle hit his first of a record 18 World Series home runs the next year in the eighth inning of Game 6 against the Dodgers and then homered again in the seventh game. He hit two more in the '53 Series and three each in 1956, '60 and '64. His homer in the ninth off Barney Schultz of the Cardinals won Game 3 of the '64 Series and broke a tie with Babe Ruth at the then Series record of 15. He hit his 17th in Game 6 and 18th, a three-run shot, in a losing seventh game. It would be the last of his 65 Series games.

Mantle, who suffered from the bone disease osteomyelitis, and was subject to muscle pulls all of his career, spent his final four years with the Yankees badly hobbled, his damaged legs wrapped from thigh to ankle in bandages. He retired in 1969 with 536 home runs, many of them among the longest ever hit. It was he, in fact, who inspired the term "tape measure shot" when, in 1953, he hit one so far over the leftfield wall in Yankee Stadium, at the 391-foot mark, that it grazed a beer sign 60 feet above the playing field, carried across Fifth Street and came to rest finally in a backyard at 434 Oakdale Street. Yankee publicity director Red Patterson rushed from the park, tape measure in hand, and calculated that the ball had traveled 565 feet.

But he may have hit balls farther. Twice he hit homers off the facade above the third deck in the old Yankee Stadium, missing by only a few feet becoming the first batter ever to hit a ball out of that towering edifice. In 1960 he hit one out of Tiger Stadium in Detroit that landed in a lumberyard across Trumball Avenue, a distance of approximately 600 feet from home plate.

Mantle hit more than 50 homers twice, 52 in 1956 and 54 in 1961, when he and teammate Roger Maris chased Ruth's record of 60. A switch-hitter, he hit home runs from both sides of the plate in the same game a record 10 times. His enormous strength came, he believed, from wielding a sledgehammer in the Oklahoma zinc mines where his father worked most of his short life. There is no accounting for the amazing speed of foot he displayed in his early seasons when he was timed running from home to first at 3.1 seconds from the right side of the plate and at three flat from the left, the fastest times ever recorded for the distance. And dragging a bunt, at which he was expert, he was clocked in an almost unbelievable 2.9 seconds. But the muscles were too mighty for his fragile bones, and his legs just couldn't support him by the late '60's.

One of Mantle's biggest disappointments was that though he hit above .300 10 times and won the Triple Crown in 1956, he finished his career with a .298 average, largely the result of those injury-marred final seasons. Still, that's not too bad for a guy who, by his own admission, "never swung at a ball I didn't try to hit out of the park."

Johnny Podres

HE WAS DEER HUNTING IN THE ADIRONDACKS NEAR his home in Witherbee, New York, when it finally dawned on Johnny Podres that he was a hero. "Hey, Podres," he called into the woods, "you beat the Yankees in the World Series! Where do you go from here, kiddo?"

Actually, the next year he went into the service, bringing him abruptly down to earth. But he came back in 1957 to win 12 games and lead the National League with a 2.66 earned run average and six shutouts. He would have a few more good years. He was 18–5 in 1961 for the now Los Angeles Dodgers, leading the league in winning percentage. And between 1957 and '64, before arm and back problems got the better of him, he won 100 games, averaging 14 wins a year. But his fame will rest forever on that 1955 World Series.

Podres had had a mediocre 9–10 season, only his third in the big leagues, and he wasn't expecting to pitch at all in the Series. But after the Dodgers dropped the first two games at Yankee Stadium, manager Walter Alston took Podres aside and advised him he would be the starter when the two teams met for the third game, at Ebbets Field. It was September 30, 1955, Podres' 23rd birthday, and he won 8–3. The Dodgers took the next two for a clean sweep in their home park, but Whitey Ford set them down 5–1 with a four-hitter on the return to Yankee Stadium. The Dodgers had yet to win a game at the Stadium in this Series and they'd yet to beat the Yankees in five previous Series tries. In fact, Brooklyn was at this point 0 for 7 in the World Series, dating back to 1916. So their prospects did not look promising.

The lefthanded Podres didn't quite see it that way. "Don't worry, Pee Wee," he said by way of consoling a downcast Reese after the Ford loss, "I'll shut 'em out tomorrow."

It seemed an idle boast until Podres started throwing. He had used a variety of pitches in beating the Yankees at Ebbets Field, relying most heavily on an effective changeup. But in the fall at Yankee Stadium there are often subtle variations of light and shadow late in the day that play across home plate. Podres decided to go with his fastball. And it was working to perfection. Gil Hodges staked him to a couple of runs with a single in the fourth and a sacrifice fly in the sixth, and that looked to be all Podres would need. But he ran into trouble in the Yankee half of the sixth when Billy Martin walked and Gil McDougald bunted for a hit. The tying runs were now on base with nobody out and the dangerous Yogi Berra at bat. To the Dodgers' surprise, Berra, a dead pull hitter, hit a looping fly ball down the leftfield line. Sandy Amoros, a defensive replacement who had been playing Berra in left center, gave chase.

"I looked around and saw the ball slicing toward the line, and I saw Amoros running his tail off," Podres recalled. "Jeez, I said to myself, he's got a hell of a run." It was "a helpless feeling standing on the mound at a moment like that." But Amoros, in a memorable World Series play, stretched out and caught the ball, and the relay from him to Reese to Hodges nailed McDougald off first for a rally-killing double play. Podres got his shutout and instant acclaim. He left the ballpark that day "surrounded by cops," so great was the crush outside. There was a big victory party with gallons of champagne that night at the Hotel Bossert in Brooklyn and later a parade though the small mining village that was his hometown (*see photo at right*), but the true measure of what he'd done didn't sink in until he got by himself in the clear crisp air of the mountains.

"Where do you go from here, kiddo?"

Don Larsen

IF ANDY WARHOL EVER REQUIRED LIVING PROOF OF HIS postulate that everyone is entitled to 15 minutes of fame, Don Larsen would be his man. Actually Larsen had two hours and six minutes of fame in a career that might otherwise charitably be described as undistinguished. This large—6' 4", 225 pounds—shambling, big-eared pitcher started with the old St. Louis Browns in 1953, ringing up a 7–12 record as a rookie. He was a horrendous 3–21 the next season as the hapless Browns moved to Baltimore and became the Orioles. He came to the Yankees in 1955 in a crowded transaction involving 18 players, the most important of whom was not Larsen but another Oriole pitcher, Bob Turley.

Larsen was 9–2 in his first season in New York but a bust in the World Series, getting shelled in his only start by the Brooklyn Dodgers for five hits and five runs in Game 4. He had another moderately successful season in 1956, winning 11 and losing five, but in his first Series start, in Game 2, he was again brutalized by the Dodgers, surviving only an inning and two thirds and blowing, in effect, a 6–0 Yankee lead. Still manager Casey Stengel had enough confidence in him to send him out for the fifth game and Warholian immortality.

There had been three World Series one-hitters up until October 8, 1956, but no one had been able to crack the no-hit barrier. And there hadn't been a perfect game in the big leagues since 1922. In 97 pitches Larsen turned both tricks. Not one Dodger reached base. Larsen was in total command, holding the 64,519 Yankee Stadium fans in his thrall. And when the 27th straight batter struck out and catcher Yogi Berra leaped like a ballerina into his arms, Larsen knew his place in baseball history was assured. And so did plate umpire Babe Pinelli, who called the last strike,

and never called another one, retiring immediately after the Series.

Larsen never won more than 10 games in a season after that. And when in 1960 the Yankees shunted him off to Kansas City, he had a miserable 1–10 year there. He was mainly a relief pitcher in his declining years, and for a variety of teams. Coincidentally he did beat the Yankees in a Series game at Yankee Stadium six years to the day after his perfect game. He was a San Francisco Giant then, and he entered Game 4 in the sixth inning in relief of Bob Bolin. Larsen pitched to two batters and got the side out in a tie game. He was lifted for a pinch hitter, Bob Nieman, in the next inning. Nieman walked to load the bases, and Giant second baseman Chuck Hiller then hit a grand slam to win the game for San Francisco. Larsen pitched only a third of an inning, but he was the winning pitcher.

He never pitched in another World Series, and he won only 12 games in the next four years before calling it a career in 1967 at the age of 38. A fiercely private man, he seemed reluctant in later years to discuss in any way his one moment in the spotlight, as if to say there must be more to life than a perfect game. He's probably right at that.

Indeed, the trouble with a Warhol sort of fame is that the deed inevitably overwhelms the performer. Mickey Owen and Fred Snodgrass had perfectly fine major league careers, but they'll forever be remembered for World Series misdeeds. Larsen crammed one crowning achievement into an otherwise unremarkable lifetime. A perfect game is a wonder to behold under any circumstances, but a perfect game pitched on the large stage of the World Series is something else again. No matter what he does with the rest of his life, Larsen must inevitably be "the guy who...." But even he would have to agree that that's better than nothing.

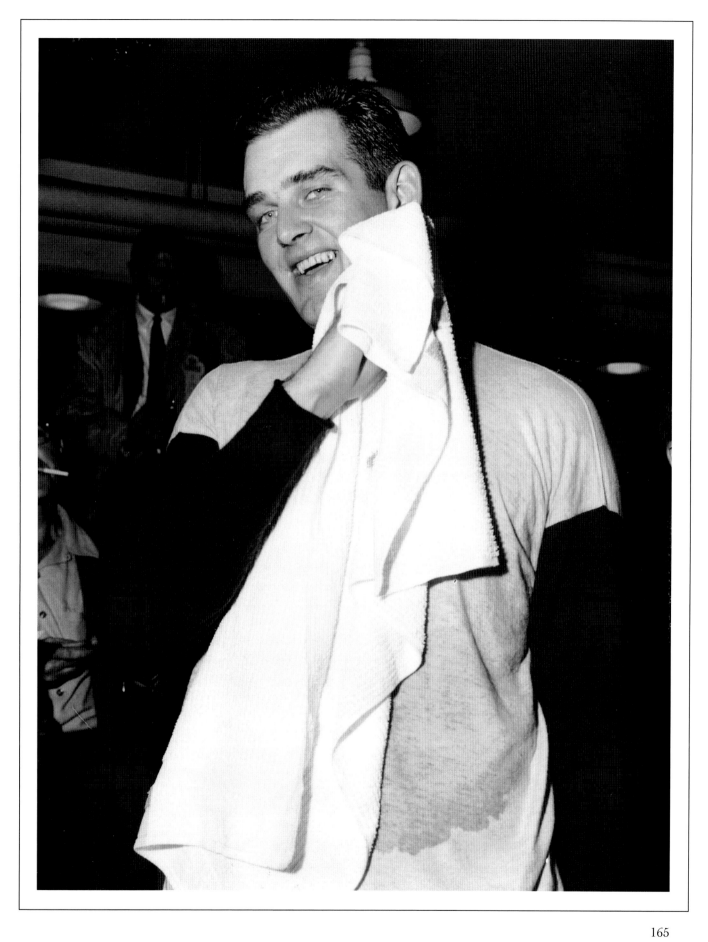

Henry Aaron

HE HAS MADE IT KNOWN NOW IN INTERVIEWS AND IN his autobiography that what should have been his proudest moment was instead an ordeal so excruciating that it plagues him yet today. His trouble actually started in 1973 when it became apparent that he, Hank Aaron, would soon pass the deified Babe Ruth as baseball's alltime home run king. Aaron had approached the record so unobtrusively, by just being his almost monotonously consistent self, that he caught many fans by surprise. But there he was, bearing down resolutely on the immortal Babe.

Aaron never hit more than 50 home runs in a season, as Ruth did four times, or 60, as Ruth did in one memorable season, but he did hit more than 30 a total of 15 times and more than 40 eight times in his 23-year career. He just seemed to play on and on, and by the time he finally called it quits in 1976, he had amassed some startling numbers in addition to the 755 home runs. He is third alltime in games played, with 3,298, trailing only Pete Rose and Carl Yastrzemski. He is second only to Rose in times at bat, with 12,364. He is, amazingly enough, tied with Ruth for second in runs scored, with 2,174, behind Ty Cobb. He is third in hits, with 3,771, behind Rose and Cobb. And he is first in runs batted in, with 2,297, 82 more than Ruth. Aaron led the National League in batting twice and in home runs and RBIs four times each. He also stole more than 20 bases six times, and finished with a total of 240 for his career.

But the home run record is the one that sticks in the mind, or with Aaron, in the craw. When the 1974 season opened in Cincinnati for the Braves, Aaron was but one shy of tying Ruth's 714. He got that homer in his first time at bat. The hate mail, viciously racist in nature, that he had been receiving for more than a year now increased accordingly. How dare he, a black man, trample on baseball's most revered statistic! His life was repeatedly threatened, and he was obliged to hire bodyguards to protect him and his family. Nevertheless, on April 8, 1974, at 9:07 p.m., before a capacity crowd of 53,775 at Atlanta–Fulton County Stadium, Aaron hit that historic homer off the Dodgers' Al Downing, ripping a fastball in a high arc toward the 385-foot sign in left centerfield and then over the fence where a clutch of Braves relief pitchers scrambled out of the bullpen in pursuit of the ball. It was finally retrieved by reliever Tom House, who even as Aaron triumphantly rounded the bases ran hysterically toward home plate holding the ball aloft.

And then Aaron hit 40 more before retiring, the last 22 in Milwaukee, back where it all started. His evil detractors did not retire with him, however, and Aaron has not yet been able to lose the bitter taste his crowning achievement has given him.

But no amount of racist hate-mongering can detract from his greatness as a player. Aaron never had the panache of a Mantle or a Mays, and he did not play in a major media center, so his records, even the big one, just sort of sneaked up on an unwary public. Hammerin' Henry didn't really even have the World Series as a showplace for his skills. He appeared in only two, both with the Milwaukee Braves, in 1957 and '58, and both against the Yankees, the first a winner, the second a loser. He hit well in both—.393 with three homers in the 1957 seven-game winning Series and .333 in the 1958 seven-game loss. In both he was his quietly efficient self. There were no "called shots," no late-inning heroics.

Henry Aaron simply played the game hard, often and extremely well. He was elected to the Hall of Fame in 1982. And his reputation will surely survive through the ages.

Ralph Terry

"YOU DON'T OFTEN GET A SECOND CHANCE TO PROVE yourself in baseball or in life," Ralph Terry once mused. But he did. He came up to the Yankees as a power pitcher in August 1956 and started three games with little success. The next year he was traded to the Kansas City Athletics, which was then virtually a Yankee farm team, and after two losing seasons there, he was returned to New York. By now he had learned a little about pitching, had, in fact, experimented with so many different deliveries that he had everyone, including manager Casey Stengel, confused. He also had a disconcerting habit of talking to the ball as if it were some sort of recalcitrant child—"Why can't I throw you where I want to?" he asked one plaintively.

Terry had his first winning season (10–8) in 1960, and Casey, though exasperated by his incessant tinkering, had enough faith in him to make him his fourth-game starter in the World Series against Pittsburgh. Terry pitched well enough but still lost to Vernon Law 3–2. He was on the mound again in the ninth inning of the wild seventh game with the score tied 9–9 and Bill Mazeroski at bat for the Pirates. Mazeroski took one pitch for a ball and then…. Better luck next time. Mazeroski's historic home run sent the city of Pittsburgh into delirium and made Terry one of the all-time Series goats.

Terry had a fine 1961 season, though, finishing 16–3 for a great Yankee team that included Yogi Berra, Mickey Mantle, Roger Maris and Moose Skowron. Pitching guru Johnny Sain had added one more pitch to Terry's ever-expanding repertoire, a hard slider, which quickly became his "out" pitch. Still, he failed again in the Series, suffering the Yankees' only loss, 6–2, to Cincinnati in five games. He had another start in the fifth game but gave up a three-run homer to Frank Robinson and was relieved by Bud Daley in the third inning of a game the Yanks would ultimately win 13–5. In two Series he now had a record of no wins, three losses and an earned run average of 5.06.

He was the staff ace in 1962, though, finishing at 23–12 and leading the league in wins, starts (39) and innings pitched (298⅔). Opponents could muster only a paltry .231 batting average against him. Now, against the San Francisco Giants, he would confront once more his Series jinx. Score one for the jinx in Game 2, the Giants' 2–0 win inflicting him with his fourth straight Series loss. But he held on to pitch a complete-game 5–3 win in Game 5 and was given the start in the seventh and final game. For eight innings he was nearly untouchable, holding the Giants scoreless and giving up just two hits. But in the last of the ninth Matty Alou led off with a bunt single, and after Felipe Alou and Chuck Hiller struck out, Willie Mays lined a double to right. Maris made a fine play on the ball, holding Alou at third. But Terry was in the soup once more, and Yankee fans were recalling the Mazeroski nightmare. Terry made good on his chance this time, although Willie McCovey hit a vicious line drive that would have been the game-winning hit had second baseman Bobby Richardson not played him perfectly.

That, unfortunately, would be the high spot of an up-and-down career. Terry had 17 wins and led the league in complete games in 1963, but pitched only three innings in relief in the Dodgers' sweep of the Yanks and then after a 7–11 season in '64 was traded to Cleveland. He finished his career "mentally divorced from the game," with the last place Mets in 1967. And then when they let him go, he retired at the age of 31. Fresh out of chances.

Sandy Koufax

OF ALL THE PITCHERS OF THAT GREAT DECADE OF pitching, the 1960s—Gibson, Ford, Marichal, Drysdale, Jenkins—one name stands apart: Sandy Koufax. For that matter Koufax must rank with Waddell, Grove, Hubbell and Spahn among the great lefthanders of baseball history. And this was a man who pitched only 12 years and was the recognizable Koufax for only six of those. When he signed with the Dodgers for a $20,000 bonus in 1955, the team had high hopes for him, but not so much for his pitching, which was then questionable, as for his potential as a gate attraction, for Koufax was not only a Brooklyn native, he was also Jewish, and Jewish ballplayers of whatever ability were at a premium in New York then. Alas, three years after he signed, the team moved to Los Angeles.

Unfortunately, as a "bonus baby," Koufax could not be sent down to the minor leagues for seasoning under rules then that required prospects receiving a bonus of more than $6,000 to remain with the big league team for two years. He pitched sparingly in his formative years, although both of his wins in '55 were by shutout. He was also apparently uncontrollably wild. In the first year he did any real pitching, 1958, he walked 105 batters in 158⅔ innings. He also struck out 131 with as wicked a fastball as had been seen—or not seen—in the league since Dizzy Dean. But what use was such a hummer if he couldn't get it over the plate? Even taking batting practice against him was, said one Dodger, "like playing Russian roulette with five bullets." Koufax pitched not an inning in the World Series of 1955 and '56.

When the team moved to Los Angeles there were some indications that he was finally emerging from his primitive state. On August 31, 1959, he tied Bob Feller's major league record by striking out 18 in a game, and since he had fanned 13 the previous game, the 31 K's gave him the record for two consecutive games. But he

was only 8–6 that year with 92 walks in 153⅓ innings. He pitched twice in the '59 World Series, losing a 1–0 game to the White Sox as a starter in Game 5. Pitching regularly in 1960, he was an unimpressive 8–13 with 100 walks in 175 innings. For his first six years in the big leagues, Koufax had only 36 wins and 40 losses.

And then miraculously it all began to come together. It had taken six years, but Koufax had finally learned to relax on the mound and harness his enormous talent. The next six years beggar description. He pitched four no-hitters, including a perfect game. He won three Cy Young Awards, this at a time when the award was given to the best pitcher in *both* leagues. He was the National League's Most Valuable Player in 1963. He won four strikeout championships, whiffing more than 300 three times and setting, in 1965, a new major league record (since broken by Nolan Ryan) of 382 in a season. He struck out 18 hitters in a game for the second time. He had winning seasons of 25–5 in '63, 26–8 in '65 and 27–9 in '66. He led the league with 27 complete games in both '65 and '66, and he won the ERA title five straight years with averages of 2.54, 1.88, 1.74, 2.04 and 1.73. For those six years he was 129–47, the last five 111–34.

In the 1963 World Series he beat the Yankees twice, establishing a new single-game strikeout record of 15 in Game 1. In 1965 he defeated the Twins twice and struck out 29 in 24 innings. He lost his only start in the Orioles' sweep of the Dodgers in '66 but gave up only one earned run. In his four World Series he had an ERA of 0.95 with 61 strikeouts in 57 innings.

And then, almost as quickly as it started, it was over. Koufax retired after the 1966 World Series with arthritis in his pitching elbow so severe he feared permanent disability. "He left at High Noon," an admirer wrote, "a Hamlet in mid-soliloquy."

Bob Gibson

HE WAS THE VERY DEFINITION OF A CLUTCH PLAYER. And certainly not one to take liberties with, for he was the most intimidating pitcher of his pitching-rich era. Gibson had a remarkable record in the World Series. After losing his first start 8–3 to the Yankees in the second game of the 1964 Series, he pitched a record seven consecutive complete-game victories in '64, '67 and '68 before losing to Mickey Lolich and Detroit in the final game of 1968, a Series in which he set strikeout records for a game (17) and a Series (35). Two of his seven wins were shutouts, and his earned run average for nine starts and 81 innings was a meager 1.89. Five times he struck out 10 batters or more in a Series game, and he finished with 92 in his 81 innings.

Of course, Gibson was a pretty fair pitcher in the regular season as well. He had won 251 games and lost 174 by the time of his retirement following the 1975 season, and with 3,117 strikeouts then, he was second only to Walter Johnson. He's now 10th on the alltime strikeout list. His 1.12 ERA for the 1968 season remains a record low for pitchers appearing in 300 or more innings. A versatile player, he won nine Gold Gloves in his career and became the first pitcher to hit two World Series home runs.

Gibson was, for that matter, an exceptional all-around athlete. An asthmatic child who grew up in a fatherless family in an Omaha ghetto, he developed a fiercely competitive nature and an uncommon will to excel. "He was pushed around as a kid," said his Cardinal teammate Mike Shannon, "and he vowed to himself that he wouldn't be pushed around again." At Creighton University in Omaha, he starred in both baseball and basketball and was good enough at hoops to tour with the Harlem Globetrotters for a year before starting his baseball career. He broke in with the Cardinals in 1959, when he was 23, but pitched rarely his first two years, mainly, he thought, because then manager Solly Hemus wasn't really sure who he was,

occasionally confusing him with shortstop Julio Gotay.

Gibson's career took off, however, when Johnny Keane replaced Hemus in 1961. He won 19 games in the championship year of 1964 and 20 and 21 the next two years. He suffered a broken leg in the 1967 season but came back to win three games in the Series that year, and he won 20 or more games in each of the next three seasons.

Gibson felt he owned the inside part of the plate, and woe betide the hitter foolish enough to challenge him there. Rookies, veterans, even former teammates all hit the dirt if they crowded the ferocious Gibby. His old teammate Lou Brock once shook his head in dismay watching the Reds' George Foster step in and out of the batter's box before finally deciding he was ready to hit. "Oh, my," said Brock, "if Gibby were still pitching and he had to wait around for all that, I'd hate to think what might happen to that poor man." Once after Pete LaCock of the Cubs homered off him, Gibson ran alongside him on the base paths, hurling epithets. When his former teammate and good friend Bill White first played against him in a Phillie uniform, Gibson sent him spinning to the dirt on the first pitch. There are no friends, he seemed to be saying, with bats in their hands.

Gibson preferred to work quickly, in contrast to the living statues who work the mound these days, and he brooked no interference from his catchers. Once when Tim McCarver started gingerly toward the mound to engage him in a strategy discussion, Gibson barked at him, "The only thing you know about pitching is that it's hard to hit. Now get out of here. … Put those fingers down as fast as you can." He also subscribed to a version of the Humphrey Bogart theory that an actor owes his public nothing more than a good performance. "I owe the fans 100 percent on the field, and I give exactly that," Gibson once said. "Anything else I give is completely up to me." In the end, he gave plenty.

Lou Brock

THE PREVAILING SENTIMENT AMONG FANS, THE PRESS and even the players on both teams was that the Cardinals made a boo-boo when, on June 15, 1964, they traded pitchers Ernie Broglio and Bobby Shantz and outfielder Doug Clemens to the Cubs for outfielder Lou Brock and pitchers Paul Toth and Jack Spring. The key players in the transaction, after all, were Brock, then 25, and Broglio, a 29-year-old righthander who had won 21 games in 1960 and 18 only the year before. In two full seasons as a Chicago Cub, Brock had hit no higher than .263 and was considered a liability in the outfield. He had stolen 24 bases in '63 but was thought of as inconsistent and unproven.

Bill White, the Cardinals' first baseman, strongly questioned the logic of trading a 20-game winner for "a guy who was very raw and didn't know how to play." Team owner Gussie Busch thought so little of the deal that he fired the general manager who made it, Bing Devine, only two months afterward. The Cards were, in fact, in seventh place when Brock joined the team, and their prospects for rising much higher, particularly with this decimation of the pitching staff, seemed unpromising at best.

So much for first impressions. As it developed, that trade may well go down in history as one of the most brilliant ever made—by the Cardinals. Broglio won only four games for the Cubs the remainder of that season and three more in a career that ended prematurely because of a sore arm two years later. Brock became the most electrifying player of his generation, a Hall of Famer who would establish new records for stolen bases in a season and a career. In fact, he paid immediate dividends for the Cards, hitting .348 in the 103 games left in the '64 season and stealing 33 bases. He sparked his new team to a dramatic come-from-behind pennant victory over the Phillies and the Reds and a

World Series win over the Yankees. Brock hit .300 in that Series with two doubles and five runs batted in.

Actually 1964 was his poorest Series. In '67, a year in which he became the first player to hit more than 20 homers (21) and steal more than 50 bases (52) in a season, he helped beat Boston in seven games by hitting .414 and stealing a World Series–record seven bases. He was 4 for 4 in Game 1 with two steals, and in the final game he stole three more bases in a 7–2 Cardinal win. In 1968, in a Series loss to Detroit, Brock shone again, tying his own stolen base record, hitting two homers and scoring six runs while hitting a heroic .464. In 21 Series games Brock hit for an average of .391, the highest ever for 20 or more games; scored 16 runs and batted in 13; and hit seven doubles, two triples and four homers.

In the 1974 season he stole 118 bases, breaking Maury Wills' record of 104, and in 1977 he surpassed Ty Cobb's career mark of 892. Brock retired after the '79 season (hitting .304) with 938 steals and 3,023 hits. He was elected to the Hall of Fame his first year of eligibility.

Brock had very little else beyond ability in common with fellow base thieves Wills, Cobb and Rickey Henderson, who eventually broke all of his records. He was a modest man, quiet and studious. A mathematics major at Southern University in Louisiana, he made a science of base stealing, calculating exactly how many steps (13) it took him to get to second base running. He played a psychological game with opposing pitchers and catchers—"They know I'm going, but they don't know when"—and he arrived at the indisputable conclusion that, "if you can't hit, you don't get on base often enough to make a reputation as a base stealer."

Raised in a poor family in rural Louisiana, Brock later enjoyed considerable success as a businessman in St. Louis. As he put it, "You have to have that quest for the final moment of glory."

Frank Robinson

HE WAS A TOUGH, AGGRESSIVE, DIFFICULT AND ABUN-
dantly talented player, the first to win the Most Valuable Player award in both leagues and the first African-
American to manage a major league team. Frank
Robinson played 21 years and had a lifetime batting
average of .294. He missed getting 3,000 hits by 57 and
600 home runs by 14. He scored 1,829 runs and batted in 1,812. He was a superb outfielder and a daring
base runner who instilled fear into the hearts of middle infielders in two leagues with his steamroller
slides into second base. He had double figures in
stolen bases for nine consecutive years, with a top of
26 in 1963.

He crowded the plate, daring pitchers to drive him
back, and he gave as good as he got. He was Rookie
of the Year in 1956, batting .290, driving in 83 runs and
tying a then record for first-year players, with 38
homers. After 10 highly productive years in Cincinnati, he was traded to Baltimore in 1966, the Reds'
management explaining to outraged fans that, though
Robinson was only 30, he was "an old 30." It turned
out he was a young 31, and he won the Triple Crown
as an Oriole in '66, hitting .316 with 49 homers and 122
runs batted in. In 1970, at age 35, he hit two grand slam
home runs in the same game.

Robinson played in five World Series. His 1961
Reds team lost to the Yankees, and in four Series
with the Orioles, he won two and lost two. He never
batted above .300 in any of them, but he did hit at least
one home run in each and two in three of them. In 26
Series games he scored 19 runs and drove in 14, while
batting a collective .250. But Robinson's true measure
as a player could never be calculated in statistics,
gaudy though most of them were. In the 1971 Series
against Pittsburgh, for example, he won the sixth
game pretty much on his own when, with the score tied

2–2 with one out in the 10th inning, he walked and then
dashed to third on a ground ball single up the middle
by Merv Rettenmund, barely beating Vic Davalillo's
throw with a belly flop slide. Then, when Brooks
Robinson hit a fly ball to shallow centerfield, he tagged
up and slid between Pirate catcher Manny Sanguillen's
legs just ahead of Davalillo's throw to score the winning run. Unfortunately he merely staved off the ultimate defeat, since the Pirates won Game 7 the next day
to complete their upset of the heavily favored Orioles.

In the 1966 sweep by the Orioles of the Dodgers,
Robinson hit a two-run homer in Game 1 to help
ensure a victory for reliever Moe Drabowsky and his
solo homer in Game 4 was the only run of the game in
Dave McNally's shutout win. In 1970, though overshadowed by the exploits of the other Baltimore Robinson, Frank nonetheless was a key contributor, hitting
two home runs, scoring five runs and driving in four in
the Orioles' five-game Series victory over the Reds.

Robinson's combination of baseball cunning and
fierce competitiveness made him a sound choice to
break down a long-standing racial barrier, and in
1975 the Cleveland Indians made him the game's
first black manager. For two years he also continued
to play in Cleveland, making him one of the few
player-managers in the modern era. He managed for
all or part of 11 seasons at Cleveland, San Francisco
and Baltimore, but none of his teams ever finished
higher than second. As a field boss Robinson experienced many of the difficulties attendant upon superstars managing inferior talent. He grew frustrated
and impatient, and his discomfort was reflected in his
attitude toward his players. As he grew older, though,
he developed a higher level of tolerance. Robinson later
graduated to the Orioles' front office. He was elected
to the Hall of Fame in 1982.

Brooks Robinson

AFTER BROOKS ROBINSON CONVERTED WHAT APPEARED to be a certain double down the leftfield line into a routine out at first base, the victimized batter, Cincinnati's Lee May, complained that the Baltimore third baseman was not so much human as "a human vacuum cleaner." Indeed, he did have the look of a household appliance in that 1970 Series when an amazed national television audience watched him suck up potential base hits as if they were so many dust balls. But as fans of the Orioles had come to know, Brooksie did that sort of thing all the time. Old-timers may hold out for Pie Traynor and younger National League fans may argue for Mike Schmidt, but most experts will declare unequivocally that in all of baseball history there has never been a third baseman to compare with Brooks Robinson.

The raw statistics, though they can scarcely capture the sheer wizardry of the man, would seem to bolster that contention. Robinson had the best career fielding average (.971) and he accepted more total chances at third (8,902) than anyone else has. He had 6,205 assists, 1,175 more than Schmidt, and 2,697 putouts, 409 more than Traynor. Robinson also leads all third basemen in double plays, with 618. He led his league's third basemen in fielding 11 times and in assists eight times, both records. And he won 16 Gold Gloves.

Robinson was not a fast runner, but he had quick reactions and great anticipation. He knew the hitters and often challenged them by playing shallow. He had a strong and accurate arm and an extraordinarily quick release. He was also ambidextrous, which may account for his unusual hand-eye coordination.

He could also hit a little. He was the American League's Most Valuable Player in 1964, when he batted .317 with 28 home runs and a league-leading 118 runs batted in. And in the 1970 Series, when he cap-

tivated the nation with his acrobatic play afield, he also hit .429 with a couple of homers and six runs batted in. The next year, when the Pirates edged the Orioles four games to three, Robinson hit .318 with five RBIs in the losing cause. He hit more than 20 homers six times in his 23-year career and finished with 268, along with 1,357 RBIs. But his career batting average was only .267, and since he was not a genuine power hitter, there is little question that he made the Hall of Fame—"a hitter's Hall"—in 1983, his first year of eligibility, on the strength of his phenomenal glovework.

Robinson was, like so many great players, supremely confident and more than a little superstitious. Smarting from the upset loss to the Mets in the 1969 Series, he affixed a tag to his luggage early in the '70 season which read: "Brooks Robinson, 1970 World Champions." Then, in no small part due to his own contributions, the Orioles became just that: world champions. Hall of Fame officials asked for his magical glove after the Series victory, and Brooks might have obliged them but for one nagging concern: What if there are a few more miracles left in that pocket? He held onto the glove for one more year.

The Arkansas-born Robinson was not only a brilliant player, he was and is—as a broadcaster—one of baseball's true gentlemen, good-humored, cooperative, insightful. The largest crowd ever to see a baseball game at Baltimore's old Memorial Stadium, 51,798, turned out for Brooks Robinson Day, on September 18, 1977, to honor the retiring 40-year-old star. Recalling his rookie year of 1955, Brooks told the crowd, "Never in my wildest dreams did I think that 23 years later I'd be standing here saying goodbye to so many people. I don't think I would want one day to change."

Lee May and hundreds of other victims of his fielding excellence might want to change a few, though.

Mickey Lolich

That plaintive cry came not from some salvaged Forgotten Man but from Mickey Lolich, a portly and robust lefthanded pitcher, immediately after the Detroit Tigers had defeated the St. Louis Cardinals in the 1968 World Series. It was a Series that began with no one much caring who or with whom Lolich was and ended with him as a national hero. He had been a 17-game winner with Detroit that year and had enjoyed five pretty fair seasons in the big leagues, but he'd scarcely rated a photo caption in the local press as his teammate Denny McLain won 31 games, becoming the first pitcher to crack 30 wins in 34 years. Lolich rode motorcycles. McLain played the organ in nightclubs. Lolich was a nice guy. McLain had wit and charm to burn. The opposing team in this World Series was not without a pitching attraction of its own—Bob Gibson, who had won 22 games for the Cardinals and set a modern major league record with his next-to-impossible earned run average of 1.12. The Series, then, was to have been all McLain and Gibson. Instead, it was all Lolich.

After Gibson beat McLain in the opener, pitching—what else?—a shutout, Lolich came on to win Game 2, 8–1, limiting the Cardinals to six hits while striking out nine. The Cards rebounded to win the next two games and needed only to beat Lolich in Game 5 to close out the Series. And Lolich started poorly, giving up three runs in the first inning on a double by Lou Brock, a run-scoring single by Curt Flood and a two-run homer by Orlando Cepeda.

But he shut them out the rest of the way as the Tigers pecked away at that lead and finally moved ahead to stay on Al Kaline's bases-loaded single in the seventh inning. The Tigers clobbered seven St. Louis pitchers in Game 6 for a Series-tying, 13–1 win.

Once more, it was up to Lolich. And this time his opponent would be Gibson.

The two were locked in a scoreless tie through six innings, Lolich snuffing out a potential Cardinal rally in the sixth by picking the two best Cardinal base runners, Brock and Flood, off first base. In the seventh the Tigers got the break they needed when, with two outs, Norm Cash and Willie Horton singled and Jim Northrup hit a drive to deep centerfield that Flood lost against the backdrop of the stands. The ball dropped for a triple that scored both Cash and Horton. Then catcher Bill Freehan doubled to left, scoring Northrup, and Lolich had all the runs he would require. Both teams scored in the ninth, but Lolich had beaten the untouchable Cardinal ace 4–1 for his third straight complete-game victory.

He had allowed only 20 hits and five earned runs in his 27 innings and had struck out 21. By beating Gibson in the Series finale, he halted the pitcher's seven-game Series winning streak. And oddly enough both he and Gibson had identical 1.67 ERAs for the Series. McLain, on the other hand, had won only one of his three starts, a result which proved to be a bad omen; he would enjoy one more good season, winning 24 games in '69, then fall prey to injury, winning just 17 more games over the next three seasons before retiring at the age of 28.

Lolich would continue pitching through the 1979 season and finish his career with a 217–191 won-loss record. He would win 19 games in 1969, record the best season of his career in '71, leading the league with 25 wins and 308 strikeouts, then win another 22 games in '72. But his reputation would forever rest on his clutch pitching in the 1968 World Series. "You all thought I was an improbable hero," he said, accurately enough, "but I came sneaking through." That he did.

Al Kaline

HE SEIZED THE LIMELIGHT WHEN HE WON A BATTING championship at the age of 20 and then gratefully slipped backstage to become a sort of perennially underrated Mr. Consistency. It took Al Kaline 16 seasons to get into a World Series, but when he finally made one, he dutifully stepped forward again, as if bored at last with his role as dependable drone. Actually it required some maneuvering by Detroit Tiger manager Mayo Smith to get the then 33-year-old star into the Series at all. Kaline had played in only 102 games in 1968, 74 in the outfield, but had hit .287. Smith had no punch at all from the shortstop position, Ray Oyler hitting only .135, Dick Tracewski .156. Confronted with a powerful Cardinal pitching staff, Smith envisioned a hitless future for the bottom of his order, so, in a daring move, he shook up his outfield, moving centerfielder Mickey Stanley to shortstop, a position he had played exactly nine times in his five-year big league career, switching rightfielder Jim Northrup to center and moving the aging and by now injury-bedeviled Kaline to right. Willie Horton would stay in left.

It was a move of pure genius. Stanley handled 31 of 33 chances cleanly and played shortstop like a veteran. And Kaline, the old war-horse, was the hitting star of the Series. In the fifth game, with the Cardinals ahead in the Series three games to one and leading in the game 3–2 after six innings, the Tigers were on the brink of extinction. But Kaline singled with the bases loaded in the seventh to drive in the tying and go-ahead runs as the Tigers finally won 5–3. With the Cardinals lead cut to three games to two, Kaline again led the way in Game 6. In a fantastic record-tying 10-run third inning, he came to bat twice, singled twice and drove in three runs. The Tigers won 13–1, knotting the Series. Then with Mickey Lolich pitching his third game, they won the finale 4–1 for their first World Series victory since 1945.

Kaline, little more than a part-time player that season, hit .379 in the only World Series of his career, belted two homers and drove in eight runs. And then he stepped quietly back into the wings. It's not that he went entirely unrecognized, for his peers considered him an almost perfect player. "He is in a very rare category," said Billy Martin. "There are a lot of good hitters in baseball and a lot of good base runners and a lot of good outfielders. But there are very few who combine everything with a good throwing arm. Al Kaline could do all those things." It's just that he did them quietly and without fuss.

He set an American League record by playing 100 or more games for 20 seasons in a 22-year career. On September 24, 1974, he became the first American Leaguer since Eddie Collins in 1925 to get 3,000 hits. And he finished that year, his last, with seven more hits. He hit home runs in double figures from 1954, his first complete season, through his last, 20 years later. The .340 he hit in his third season was his highest average, but he hit above .300 nine times and finished with a lifetime average of .297. He scored 1,622 runs and drove in 1,583 and hit 498 doubles and 399 homers. He hit 29 homers in a season twice and 27 four times. He was a positively flawless rightfielder with a powerful and accurate throwing arm. In 1971, when he was 36, he played 129 errorless games in the outfield. He was elected to the Hall of Fame in 1980, his first year of eligibility.

Kaline came from a working-class family in Baltimore and was signed by the Tigers right out of high school. He never displayed anything resembling ego and was content to remain with the same team throughout his baseball life. Criticism hurt, but he took it in stride. "I really don't care what people say," he once said. "Self-centered people are the only ones who worry about what other people say about them."

Al Kaline had no worries.

Roberto Clemente

HE HAD WON FOUR BATTING CHAMPIONSHIPS BEFORE the 1971 World Series, but Roberto Clemente had played much of his exemplary career in the large shadows cast by such glamorous stars of the 1960s as Willie Mays, Mickey Mantle, Hank Aaron, Frank Robinson and Roger Maris. In the relative seclusion of Pittsburgh, though, he had been accumulating the impressive statistics that would leave him with an even 3,000 hits and a lifetime batting average of .317 by the time of his last game in 1972. He may also have been the best defensive rightfielder, with speed and a cannon arm, ever to play the game. But it was the 1971 Series that finally brought him stage center.

Clemente had hit .310 in the Pirates' upset of the Yankees in 1960, but that Series will forever belong to Bill Mazeroski. He would have 1971 as his alone. The Pirates were given little chance of beating the mighty Orioles with their pitching staff of multiple 20-game winners, their airtight defense and the slugging of the Robinsons, Frank and Brooks, and Boog Powell, especially after Baltimore won the first two games. Surveying this initial damage, Pittsburgh's Willie Stargell was moved to comment, "You would have thought the Pittsburgh Pirates were nothing more than the invited guests at the St. Valentine's Day Massacre."

Clemente was 37 then and presumably past his prime. But he hit safely in every game, batted .414 with two doubles, a triple and two homers. And he thrilled a nationwide television audience with his spectacular play in the outfield. Driven on by his masterful play, the Pirates overcame the two-game disadvantage and whipped the Orioles in seven games. Clemente's fourth-inning homer into the centerfield bleachers in the climactic game gave Pirate starter Steve Blass the momentum he needed to eke out a 2–1 win. Clemente so dominated play that whenever he came to bat in Pittsburgh's Three Rivers Stadium, the house organist played "Jesus Christ Superstar."

A proud Latino unusually sensitive to perceived slights, Clemente rejoiced in his newfound celebrity. In the past, because of a chronically bad back, he had been rapped as a world-class hypochondriac. Now he was acclaimed as a gritty comeback artist. "It's a shame," said Pirate pitcher Dave Giusti years later, "that it took the 1971 World Series before people said, 'Hey, this guy is one of the greatest ever to put on a uniform.'"

It *is* a shame, because Clemente had only one more year to live. Two days before Christmas in 1972, Nicaragua was shaken by a severe earthquake that left 5,000 dead and thousands more homeless. Clemente, who had played winter ball there, became chairman of the Nicaraguan relief drive in his native Puerto Rico, and he worked 14-hour days helping collect food and clothing for the quake victims. On New Year's Eve he boarded a DC–7 cargo plane carrying supplies to the stricken country from the airport in San Juan, Puerto Rico. The plane—haphazardly loaded, it was revealed later—crashed at sea not two miles from the airport, killing all four aboard. Clemente's body was never found, although divers, including his teammate Manny Sanguillen, searched the Atlantic depths for days afterward. He left a wife and three small sons.

In his lifetime Clemente may not have received the recognition he justly deserved, but in death he has become a hero. He was elected posthumously to the Hall of Fame in 1973, the five-year retirement rule duly waived in his case. Two hospitals in Puerto Rico have been named for him as well as the 400-acre, $13 million Roberto Clemente Sports City Complex. And a statue was dedicated outside Three Rivers Stadium on August 18, 1994, which would have been his 60th birthday.

Rollie Fingers

HE MAY NOT HAVE EXACTLY REVOLUTIONIZED RELIEF pitching, but he certainly perfected the craft and gave new stature to the long-neglected bullpen ace. He was an imposing figure striding in from the pen, long and lean and with a bristling Mephistophelian mustache that made him resemble a Prussian officer. But Rollie Fingers was all quiet efficiency on the mound, coolly dispatching hitters with his hard slider and pinpoint control. He was the closer and much more for Charlie Finley's three-time world champion Oakland A's of the early '70's, and his total of six saves, two each in the World Series of 1972, '73 and '74, remains a record. He pitched in 16 Series games, a total of 33⅓ innings with 25 strikeouts and only 10 walks. His earned run averages were 1.74, 0.66 and 1.93, and his one win and two saves in the five-game win over the Dodgers in 1974 earned him that Series' Most Valuable Player honors.

Fingers was very much a part of the roistering knock-about scene under Finley in those years. He was not the first on the team to grow a mustache, though. That distinction belongs to Reggie Jackson, who showed up unshaven for spring training in 1972. Fingers and his bullpen mates Bob Locker and Darold Knowles were so taken with Reggie's new hirsute look that they set about growing mustaches of their own. Finley went along with the gag and offered $300 to any of his players who could grow acceptable facial hair by Father's Day. The entire team, including manager Dick Williams, collected. But Fingers, with a handlebar job that would have done Kaiser Wilhelm proud, was the acknowledged champion. One year Finley included as part of a minimal wage increase for his star reliever a year's supply of mustache wax. Fingers repaid him with 27 wins and 61 saves in the three championship seasons, this at a time when saves were not so easily come by as under more sophisticated contemporary rules.

The A's in those years were as renowned for their clubhouse brawling as for their play afield, and Fingers, a team man all the way, was a willing participant in these extracurricular tussles. The day before the start of the '74 Series, he and starting pitcher John (Blue Moon) Odom settled an argument by slamming into each other, Fingers emerging with a lacerated scalp, Odom with a sprained ankle. Earlier that same year, when Jackson and centerfielder Billy North had at each other in another clubhouse dustup, Fingers shrugged and said, "So what else is new? Being on this club is like having a ringside seat for the Muhammad Ali–Joe Frazier fights."

As a free agent following the 1976 season, Fingers left the A's for more tranquil surroundings in San Diego, where he led the National League with 35 and 37 saves in '77 and '78. During the decade of the '70s, he appeared in more games (660) than any other pitcher and had more saves (209) than any other reliever. He spent four seasons with the Padres, averaging nine wins and 27 saves a year, and then in a complicated transaction involving the Cardinals, for whom he never pitched, he landed in Milwaukee. And in the strike-truncated season of 1981 he led the American League with 28 saves and had an earned run average of 1.04 in 47 games. He won both the American League Cy Young and Most Valuable Player awards that year. A torn muscle in his right forearm kept him out of the 1982 World Series and painful tendinitis in his right elbow caused him to miss the entire 1983 season, but he returned in 1984 to save 23 games for the Brewers.

Fingers retired after the 1985 season with a major league record, since broken, of 341 saves. He was elected to the Hall of Fame in 1992, only the second relief pitcher (Hoyt Wilhelm was the first) so honored.

Reggie Jackson

HE WAS MR. OCTOBER. THE "STRAW THAT STIRS THE drink." And to some of his teammates, managers and owners, Mr. Obnoxious. But Reggie Jackson, perhaps more than any player since the Babe himself, had an innate sense of drama and an uncanny way of performing at his best when the spotlight was shining brightest upon him. When he finally retired in 1987 after a 21-year career, he had hit 563 home runs, sixth on the alltime list, and driven in 1,702 runs, 17th alltime. He had also set a new major league record by striking out 2,597 times, the only slugger among the top 15 home run hitters with more strikeouts than base hits. No whiffer in history is, in fact, within 600 K's of this futility standard. Then again, Reggie always had a tendency to go too far. And if teammates chafed at his publicity, at his garrulity or his egocentricity, it was a burden, like the strikeouts, that he bore cheerfully.

In the beginning he was a complete player, a power hitter who could run the bases and catch a fly ball even if he at first misjudged it. In the end he was strictly one-dimensional, a guy who could hit the ball out of the lot but couldn't be counted on for much else. He broke in with the Kansas City Athletics late in the 1967 season and moved with the team to Oakland the next year. In 1969 he caught national attention for the first time by hitting 47 homers. He also became involved in an ongoing feud with his even more egocentric owner, Charles O. Finley. With Finley sniping at him and underpaying him, Reggie slumped to just 23 homers and a .237 batting average in 1970. But, like all the A's, he learned to cope with his crotchety boss, and he helped lead the team in the next few years to three straight world titles. Jackson missed the 1972 World Series with a torn hamstring, but he drove in a total of seven runs in the next two Series, against the Mets and the Dodgers. He and Finley finally parted company after the 1975 season, Reggie moving on as a free agent to Baltimore and then to New York and everlasting fame as George Steinbrenner's Mr. October. Reggie, who had been feuding all season with manager Billy Martin, hit a resounding .450 in the 1977 Series win by the Yankees over the Dodgers and broke or tied eight records. He hit five home runs in just six games. He tied Willie Stargell for most total bases, with 25. He became the only player besides the Babe to hit three homers in a game. And he scored a record 10 runs in the Series and tied the record for most runs in a game, with four.

What he accomplished in that sixth and final game may never be approached, for he hit three straight home runs off three straight pitches thrown by three different pitchers. In the fourth inning he hit, as he called it, a "hook shot" into the lower bleachers in rightfield off Burt Hooton with a runner on. In the fifth he hit another two-run shot deep to right center off reliever Elias Sosa. These four RBIs gave the Yankees an insuperable 7–3 lead, but the coup de grace was yet to come. "All I had to do was show up at the plate," Jackson modestly recalled. "They were going to cheer me even if I struck out." Indeed, the "Reg-ee, Reg-ee, Reg-ee" chants had hit a maniacal pitch by the time of his last at bat. The Dodger pitcher was Charlie Hough, a hard-to-hit knuckleballer. Hough threw one pitch, and Jackson hit a cloud-buster that finally descended onto the black tarpaulin in dead centerfield, some 450 feet from home plate. "Reg-ee, Reg-ee, Reg-ee!" "Hey, man, it's three," said Reg as he bounded around the bases amid bedlam.

Jackson entertained his namesake, the Reverend Jesse Jackson, in his Fifth Avenue apartment the day after this historic game. "Reggie has a sense of moment," said Jesse, who should know of such things. "I think that's why he gets up for the big games. Greatness against the odds is the thing."

Johnny Bench

A SUREFIRE WAY OF BRINGING A HOT STOVE LEAGUE discussion to a boil is to argue the merits of the game's greatest catchers. That will fire up the Bill Dickey stalwarts. The Mickey Cochrane aficionados. The Gabby Hartnett disciples. The Roy Campanella followers. The Yogi Berra loyalists. And maybe even a few graybeard Ray Schalk diehards. Not to mention the Johnny Bench come-latelies.

Bench entered the competition in a big way when as a mere stripling of 22 in 1970 he hit 45 homers (38 while working behind the plate) and drove in 148 runs to lead the National League in both departments. He was the league's Most Valuable Player that year, and there was already talk about readying his plaque for Cooperstown. Two years later he again led the league in homers (40) and RBIs (125) and captured his second MVP award. The plaque was ready for polishing by then. And two years after that he again led in RBIs, with 129, and hit 33 homers. Why bother with the vote?

In 11 of his 17 big league seasons, Bench hit more than 20 homers, and six times he drove in more than 100 runs, remarkable figures for a catcher. He hit 389 home runs in his career, a National League record 327 as a catcher. But Bench was much more than just an offensive player. He set a major league record for rookies by catching 154 games in 1969, and he holds the league record of catching 100 games or more in 13 consecutive seasons. He had a strong arm that runners were seldom willing to challenge, and employing the one-handed catching style made possible by the new webbed mitts and pioneered by the Cubs' Randy Hundley in the early '60s, he was an expert at digging pitches out of the dirt. Catching 121 games in 1975, he did not have a passed ball. His manager at Cincinnati, Sparky Anderson, proclaimed him the best catcher he'd ever seen, and though Sparky was given to superlatives, there were many baseball men who agreed with him.

The only rap against Bench was that in his entire career he caught only one 20-game winner, Jim Merritt in 1970, while his competitors for best-ever handled giants. Dickey, after all, had Ruffing and Gomez. Cochrane had Earnshaw and Grove. Hartnett had, at one time or another, Grover Cleveland Alexander, Charlie Root and Lon Warnecke. Campy had Newcombe, Erskine and Roe. And Berra had Reynolds, Raschi and Whitey Ford. But Anderson's Captain Hook managerial style was not conducive to 20-game seasons. A Red starter in his time was lucky to finish five innings before Sparky started pulling fresh bodies out of the pen. The so-called aces of his championship teams of 1975 and '76 never won more than 15 games in a season. Catching for these Reds, Bench dealt more in quantity than quality.

Johnny was generally at his best competing head to head against other top catchers. In the 1976 World Series the Yankees' Thurman Munson played spectacularly, hitting .529 and finishing with a record-tying six straight hits. Bench topped him, hitting .533 for the Series. And he came close to winning the last game all by himself. In the fourth inning, with the score tied 1–1, he hit a two-run homer that gave the Reds a lead they never lost. And then in the ninth he hit a three-run shot that put the game out of sight. He drove in five of his team's eight runs in the game that won the Series.

Beset by injuries and contemplating the prospect of a promising new career in broadcasting, Bench retired after the 1983 season. And in his first year of eligibility, 1989, he was, as expected, elected to the Hall of Fame, only the 12th catcher so honored. The others there may rest assured they are in good company.

Pete Rose

HIS LIFE AND CAREER HAVE ALL OF THE BASIC ELEMENTS of Aristotelian poetics—the great man brought down by a tragic flaw. Pete Rose achieved wonders in baseball. In a 24-year career he was in more games (3,562), came to bat more often (14,053) and had more hits (4,256) than anyone who ever played the game. His 746 career doubles leads the National League and is second only to Tris Speaker's 793 in the major leagues. His 3,215 singles is a record. His 10 seasons with 200 hits or more surpasses Cobb's nine. With 2,165 runs scored, he is first in the National League, fourth overall. He led the NL in hits seven times, second only to Cobb's eight in the American League. He had 14 seasons in which he hit .300 or better. His 44-game hitting streak in 1978 equaled Willie Keeler's NL record and is second only to Joe DiMaggio's 56-gamer. He won three batting titles, was Rookie of the Year in 1963, MVP in the National League in '73 and MVP in the '75 Series.

As the leadoff hitter he was the ignition key of Cincinnati's Big Red Machine. Everything started with him, as witness his play in the seventh game of the '75 Series. He was on first base in the sixth inning with one out when Johnny Bench hit what seemed to be a certain double-play ball to Red Sox shortstop Rick Burleson. Second baseman Denny Doyle took Burleson's feed for one out, but Rose slid into him with such force that his relay throw to first went awry and Bench reached second on the error. Tony Perez then hit a home run to close the score to 3–2. Without Rose's slide he would not have had the chance. Rose's single in the seventh then scored Ken Griffey Sr. with the tying run, and in the ninth Joe Morgan's single won the game and the Series for the Reds.

Rose was with the Phillies in 1980 when they won the first World Series in the history of the franchise, and again he played a vital role. The Phils were ahead 4–1 in the ninth inning of Game 6, but Kansas City had the bases loaded with only one out when Frank White hit a pop foul between first base and home. When catcher Bob Boone had the ball pop out of his mitt, Rose alertly picked off the rebound before the ball touched the ground. Tug McGraw then struck out Willie Wilson to bring the championship home to Philadelphia.

His World Series play was typical of the intensity Rose brought to every game. Rose, in fact, once remarked that he would "go through hell in a gasoline suit to play baseball." No one, not even Cobb, was ever more *into* a game than Pete Rose. Cobb actually became something of an obsession with Rose as he closed in on that fiery ancient's total hit record of 4,191. When he finally got his 4,192nd on September 11, 1985, as a player-manager in his hometown of Cincinnati, there was national rejoicing. And Rose said afterward, "Clear in the sky, I see my dad, Harry Francis Rose, and Ty Cobb. Ty Cobb was in the second row. Dad was in the first."

But Rose had another obsession—gambling—and it would finally bring him down among the mortals. He had always been a heavy bettor, but in the '80s it had gone well beyond that. Investigators from the baseball commissioner's office filed a report saying there was solid evidence that Rose bet not only on baseball but on his own team's games, a crime punishable by lifetime expulsion. And on August 31, 1989, commissioner A. Bartlett Giamatti handed down his ruling: Rose was banished for life from the game that had been his life. Less than a year later Rose pleaded guilty in federal court to two counts of filing false income tax returns, another sorry aspect of his gambling addiction, and was sentenced to five months in a minimum security institution. And the Hall of Fame committee declared him ineligible for consideration as a candidate for Cooperstown.

How suddenly a life can change.

Willie Stargell

HE WAS ONE OF THE GREAT POWER HITTERS OF HIS time, but his value to his team was, if anything, more spiritual than physical, for Wilver Dornel Stargell was a natural leader. It was a gift few recognized when he was growing up dirt poor in a government housing project in Alameda, California. But when a passerby asked young Willie one day why he spent so much time hitting rocks with a stick, the boy replied that someday the rocks would be baseballs and the stick a bat and that he would be doing his hitting then in a big league stadium. And so he did. Stargell hit 475 home runs in his 21-year career, all with Pittsburgh, and some of them were colossal.

He played his first 7½ years in Forbes Field, with its 408-foot power alley in right center, so not all of his long hits reached the seats. But he did hit seven balls over the rightfield roof there and onto the street beyond, and in the entire history of that park, only 18 homers were hit that far, the first by Babe Ruth. When the Pirates moved to Three Rivers Stadium, Stargell became the first to reach the yellow seats in the third deck over rightfield, and he did it four times. He was the first and only man to hit a ball completely out of Dodger Stadium.

He hit a league-leading 48 homers in the Pirates' world-championship season of 1971 but was not much of a factor, hitting a mere .208, in his team's seven-game win over the Orioles in the Series. He more than compensated for that defective performance when the two teams met again eight years later, batting .400 and, at age 38, setting Series records for total bases (25) and extra-base hits (seven). In Game 7 he was 4 for 5 with two doubles and a two-run homer that put the Pirates ahead to stay in a 4–1 win. For the Series he scored once and batted in seven runs and hit four doubles and three homers.

But to the Pirates he was more than just another slugger; he was Pops, the paterfamilias of a heterogeneous "family." *(He is pictured at right with his daughter Kelli, a member of his other family.)* The Pirates had 15 blacks and Hispanics on their 25-man roster, but Stargell was a father confessor to all the races, the kindly teacher who passed out gold stars for good performances and the genial ringmaster who kept the troops loose in times of stress. But easygoing as he seemed, Stargell yet burned with a fierce competitiveness that was recognized by all. In the playoff victory over Cincinnati in 1979, he was just as dominant as in the Series, hitting the three-run homer that won Game 1 in the 11th inning and driving in a pair of runs in the pennant clinching 7–1 victory in Game 3. Overall he hit .455 with two homers and six RBIs. He was the Most Valuable Player in both the playoffs and the World Series.

In the three seasons remaining to him before he retired in 1982, Stargell never played more than 74 games and the Pirates never finished higher than third in their division. As he declined, so did his team, until finally there was no one to replace him and his unique combination of talent and leadership. But his popularity never waned.

Stargell has endeared himself to proud but defensive Pittsburghers by choosing to live year-round in their oft-maligned city. He was as familiar a figure around town as any of Pittsburgh's favorite sons, including Art Rooney and Billy Cohn. He became a "Pittsburgh guy," and the citizens loved him for it.

Throughout his long and productive career Willie Stargell held steadfast to a single philosophical notion: "If you respect this game and do what you're supposed to do, it's very rewarding. But you have to respect what you do." That was the ultimate source of his success.

Mike Schmidt

MIKE SCHMIDT WAS THAT RARE COMBINATION OF A mighty home run hitter who was also a spectacular defensive player. He led the National League in home runs a record eight times, second only to Babe Ruth's 12 homer titles in the American League. He also won 10 Gold Gloves, a National League record for third basemen. He was actually different players at bat and in the field. Schmidt the hitter was a methodical craftsman forever tinkering with his stance and his swing. Schmidt the fielder was daring and improvisational, famous for diving stops and lightning throws and for plays out of the ordinary. Once he followed his own wild throw across the diamond and made the putout himself at first base, receiving a return throw from the first baseman and tagging a runner who had overrun the bag. He was a model of consistency, though, at the plate, hitting 30 or more homers in 13 of his 16 complete seasons. On April 17, 1976, he tied a major league record by hitting four consecutive homers in one game. In 18 seasons, all with the Philadelphia Phillies, he hit 548 home runs, placing him seventh on the alltime homer list.

Schmidt had his most rewarding season in 1980. He led the league with 48 homers, belting the last four in the final four games of the season, the last giving the Phillies the division championship in an 11-inning win over Montreal. He also led the league with 121 runs batted in and a .624 slugging percentage. Powered by Schmidt, the Phillies defeated the Astros in the playoffs that year to win their first pennant since 1950. And then, with Schmidt hitting .381 with a pair of homers and seven RBIs, they beat Kansas City to win their first World Series in the then 97-year history of the franchise. In the pivotal fifth game, Schmidt hit a two-run homer to open the scoring and later scored the game-winning run in the 4–3

Phillie victory. In two previous Series, in 1915 and '50, the Phils had won only one of nine Series games. This time they beat the Royals in six, provoking a joyous, even riotous civic celebration. Schmidt was voted both the National League's Most Valuable Player that year, the first of three MVP awards he would win, and the Most Valuable Player in the World Series.

In 1983 he again led the Phillies to the National League pennant, hitting a league-leading 40 homers and driving in 109 runs, but both he and his team were sorry disappointments in a Series they lost in five games to Baltimore. Schmidt had only one hit, a single, in 20 times at bat, a rare failure for a man who thrived in pressure situations. He won his last home run and RBI championships (37 and 119) in 1986, when he was 37 years old. He hit 35 homers and drove home 113 runs the next year, then declined precipitously. He played in only 108 games in 1988 and hit just 12 homers. And after playing 42 games the next year, he ceremoniously announced his retirement.

For all of his flashy play afield and dramatic power hitting, Schmidt was a reluctant public figure who until late in his career was not comfortable with the adulation he received. An intelligent man with a degree in business administration from Ohio University, he took his game seriously and had little patience with the hoopla attending it. "It has always been uncomfortable for me to go out in public," he said in 1982. But in time he made peace with his public and willingly accepted a much larger role in community life outside baseball. And he remains, in all probability, the most popular Phillie of them all. Schmidt accepts this, too, as a responsibility.

"If a kid has a Mike Schmidt poster in his bedroom," he once said, "I'd want his parents to be happy as hell about it."

George Brett

IN 1992, HIS 20TH SEASON, GEORGE BRETT BECAME the 18th player in major league history to get 3,000 hits. He undoubtedly would have reached that milestone sooner had he been able to keep his strong but unusually vulnerable body intact for any length of time. But between 1977 and '92 Brett missed a total of 401 games because of injuries, the equivalent of 2½ seasons. He had been on the disabled list 10 times, quite possibly a record, and endured injuries to his heel, toe, ankle, knees, ribs, back, hand, wrist and shoulder. And between the second and third games of the 1980 World Series, he had a hemorrhoid operation, and then with the pain, as he put it, "behind me," hit a home run in his first time at bat in Game 3. Brett was as resilient as he was fragile.

Although he was for many years Kansas City's self-styled Bachelor King—"People knew they could find me out on the town until the bars closed"—he didn't get hurt so often because he was out of shape but because, shades of Ty Cobb and Pete Rose, he played so hard. As one team official said, "They should put just one sentence on his tombstone: 'He ran 'em all out.'" Indeed, few big leaguers have ever played the game with such unrestrained gusto, racing to first base after hitting routine grounders, converting singles into doubles, sliding violently into every base and, when he was a third baseman, hurling himself onto Royals Stadium's unforgiving artificial turf in pursuit of ground balls. "He's a blue-collar player," said Royal vice-president Dean Vogelaar. In the age of multi-millionaire athletes, Brett was a welcome link to the game's hell-for-leather past. He didn't use batting gloves (except in batting practice). He didn't wear his uniform trousers so low you couldn't see his socks. He almost never turned down interviews, and he never ever appeared nonchalant on a ball field.

He was also indisputably one of the finest players of his time. He is the only hitter to win batting championships in three different decades—.333 in 1976, .390 in '80 and .329 in '90. His .390 was the closest to .400 anyone has come since Ted Williams hit .406 in 1941. He missed much of the first half of that 1980 season with injuries and was hitting in the .240's in the first weeks of his return to action, and then he caught fire, hitting in 30 consecutive games from July 18 to August 18 at a .467 pace. By driving home 118 runs in 117 games that same year, he became only the 17th player to have more than 100 RBIs and average more than one per game. His slugging percentage of .664 in '80 was the highest in the American League since Mickey Mantle's .687 in 1961. And in 1979 he became only the fifth player to hit 20 or more homers (23), triples (20) and doubles (42).

In 1980 he led the Royals to their first American League pennant, his seventh-inning upper-deck homer off Goose Gossage beating the Yankees in the final game of the league playoffs. And in the World Series he hit .375 in a losing cause. In 1985, a season in which he hit .335 with 30 homers and 112 RBIs and won a Gold Glove, he again led the Royals into the World Series, this time against the cross-state St. Louis Cardinals. Brett hit .370 as the Royals came back from losing the first two games at home to win in seven. He was 4 for 5 in the 11–0 final game. With 10 hits and four walks in that Series, he had an on-base percentage of .452. That is, to date, the Royals' only world championship.

George Brett turned 40 in 1993, but his adoring fans still knew where to find him—at home with his wife, Leslie, whom he married in February 1992. The old haunts suffered without him, but the Bachelor King had finally abdicated.

Jack Morris

JACK MORRIS'S RECORD OF NEVER HAVING PITCHED for a losing team in the World Series remains intact, though his own string of near-flawless performances was abruptly snapped in 1992. But then again, who can say he won't be lured out of retirement to start with yet another team? World Series or no, Morris has been one of the finest pitchers of the past 20 years, the winningest of all (162 wins) in the decade of the '80s with the Tigers and a big winner in the '90s with three teams. Now comfortably retired, Morris finished his career with a superb record of 237 wins and 168 losses.

Morris's most effective weapon was the split-fingered fastball, a pitch he perfected under the tutelage of split-finger guru Roger Craig in the early '80s, when Craig was the Tigers' pitching coach. Morris bamboozled the Padres with that drop pitch in the 1984 Series, recording complete-game wins in two of the five games and becoming the first starter for manager Sparky Anderson ever to pitch a complete Series game.

In the opener, which he won 3–2, Morris was in serious difficulty only in the sixth inning, when the Padres had two men on base with no outs. He extricated himself from that jam by striking out, in order, Bobby Brown, Carmelo Martinez and Garry Templeton. Afterward he wondered out loud if even Babe Ruth and Ty Cobb could have hit his favorite pitch. "Hey," he concluded, "if Ruth and Cobb couldn't have hit the splitfinger, what chance did Martinez and Brown have?"

Morris was a strutting peacock on the mound in those days and often intolerant of his teammates' mistakes. Once in 1984 his catcher, Lance Parrish, felt compelled to admonish him: "Nobody likes to play behind you when you're this way." Even Craig accused him of "acting like a baby." "Yes, he is arrogant," argued Anderson, "but he's like a high-strung racehorse, a great thoroughbred who'll bite you if you come near him."

Morris toned down his egotism somewhat, particularly after he left the Tigers in 1991 for a tearful homecoming with the Minnesota Twins. He had grown up in St. Paul and often had said that he wanted to finish up his career back in the Twin Cities. And, at age 36, he won 18 games to lead the Twins to an American League pennant and a thrilling victory over the Atlanta Braves in the World Series. Morris won two games in the playoffs, then went seven-plus innings in the opening game of the Series, holding the Braves to five hits in a 5–2 win. In Game 4 he allowed one run in six innings but received no decision in the Twins' 3–2 loss. He was at his most dominant, though, in Game 7. Locked in a pitching duel for seven innings with the Braves' John Smoltz, Morris continued to pitch shutout ball into the 10th, when the Twins finally scored the only run of the game on Gene Larkin's single. He walked two, struck out eight and allowed only seven hits in one of the truly magnificent pitching exhibitions in Series history.

Casting sentiment aside, Morris left Minnesota for Toronto the next season, and again he led a team to an American League pennant and a World Series and became, with his 21 wins, the Blue Jays' first 20-game winner. In his two previous Series, Morris had started five games, won four, lost none, pitched three complete games and allowed seven earned runs in 41 innings. Those numbers went sadly askew in '92. In Game 1 he started well enough, shutting out Atlanta on only one hit through five innings. But in the sixth he gave up three hits, including a three-run homer by Damon Berryhill. He lost 3–1. And then in Game 5 the Braves scored seven runs off him, four coming on Lonnie Smith's grand slam in the fifth. Morris had given up 10 runs in 10⅔ innings in suffering his first two World Series losses. But the Jays recovered and won anyway in six games. Good or bad, Morris remained a winner.

Kirby Puckett

AT 5' 8" AND 218 POUNDS, HE WAS BUILT LIKE A PACKING crate, and he was so doggedly cheerful that it was hard to imagine him meaning any harm, but Kirby Puckett established himself as one of the most dangerous hitters in the game. And he was, in fact, one of the finest all-around players of the past several decades and in all probability the most lethal home field Game 6 player in World Series history.

Puckett was just a .200 hitter going into the sixth game of the 1987 Series between the Twins and the St. Louis Cardinals. But he was 4 for 4 in that game with four runs scored and one batted in as his team pounded the Cards 11–5. And he was 2 for 4 with a double and another RBI as the Twins wrapped up the Series the following day with a 4–2 win on the strength of a solid pitching performance from Frank Viola. This was the first World Series triumph for the transplanted franchise since the Washington Senators and Walter Johnson defeated the New York Giants and Frankie Frisch in 1924. Puckett hit .357 for the Series with a team-high 10 hits.

He was a sleeping little giant again in 1991 against Atlanta, with just three hits in 18 at bats and a single RBI entering the revivifying Game 6. Since, as in '87, the Twins hadn't won a single game on the road, they were trailing in the Series, three games to two, when Puckett decided to take charge. His triple in the first inning scored Chuck Knoblauch to give Minnesota a 1–0 lead. In the third he leaped against the fence in left center to take an extra-base hit away from the Braves' Ron Gant. And then in the 11th inning, with the score tied 3–3, his leadoff home run won the game and tied the Series. He was on base with an intentional walk in the 10th inning of Game 7 the next day when pinch-hitter Gene Larkin won the World Series for the home team with a single over a drawn-in outfield, which scored a jubilant Dan Gladden from third base.

Puckett hit only .250 in the 1991 Series, but included among his six hits were a triple and two home runs. He also walked five times—four times intentionally—and drove in four runs, tying him with Chili Davis for the team lead. In his two World Series he hit for an average of .308 with a double, two triples, two homers, seven walks, nine runs scored and seven driven in. In the two dramatic Game 6's, he was an astonishing 7 for 8.

Puckett was one modern athlete who preferred playing his career in one place, a predilection confirmed by his signing in late 1992 of a five-year $30-million contract to remain with the Twins. He almost certainly could have received more money had he chosen to go elsewhere. All this made him enormously popular in the Twin Cities, as well he should have been. He made his debut with the Twins on May 8, 1984, by getting four hits in a game against the California Angels. He failed to hit a home run in his rookie season, but two years later hit 31, the first time any player with more than 500 at bats in the two seasons has gone from zero to more than 30 homers. He led the American League in hits four times, the last in 1992. He was the league's batting champion in 1989 with a .339 average and was second to Seattle's Edgar Martinez in 1992 with .329. He hit above .300 in seven of his 12 seasons. From 1984 through '92 he averaged .321 with 16 homers and 13 stolen bases. And he was a perennial winner of the Gold Glove for his oustanding play in centerfield.

Sadly, Puckett was forced to retire after the 1995 season due to irreversible damage to his right eye. But he left the game with a Hall of Fame resume: .318 average, 2,304 hits, 207 home runs, two World Series rings and a history of playing his best in big games.

Future

CAMDEN YARDS: A BOW TO THE PAST THAT BODES WELL FOR BASEBALL'S FUTURE.

Baseball's present is so muddled it has become even more difficult than usual to make any sense of that unexplored world of tomorrow. And yet, amid all of the financial, structural and labor turmoil cur-

rently afflicting the game, there are some encouraging developments that bode well for the days ahead.

Baltimore's Camden Yards, for one, has restored faith in the future of baseball

architecture, a craft dishonored in the 1960s and early '70s by the erection of all those symmetrical look-alike multipurpose "stadiums." Ballpark building had been until that regrettable period a respectable

American art form. The classic parks built early in the century were fashioned to fit the game. The seats were close to the field so the players could be identified as recognizable human beings, not, as in the newer parks, dimly seen as remote and faceless figurines. The fences were at irregular distances from home plate, mainly to conform to surrounding streets, but that feature gave each ballpark a distinctive character. The Polo Grounds had its short foul lines and vast centerfield; Ebbets Field, its indented rightfield fence; the old Yankee Stadium, its death valley in left center; Crosley Field, its outfield hillock; Baker Bowl, its towering tin wall in right. These parks had personality, a quality sadly lacking in so many of today's cookie-cutter monstrosities. Can anyone say how Veterans Stadium differs from Riverfront, or Three Rivers from Busch?

But baseball architects are now looking to the past for the future. Camden Yards has proved that neoclassicism works, that a ballpark itself can be a gate attraction. More parks blending the old look with modern conveniences have been built in Cleveland, Arlington (Texas) and Denver. No one has any trouble telling them apart. And all of them, it is profoundly to be appreciated, have fields of natural grass. There seems little reason now for any more of those abominable artificial surfaces except in the equally abominable domed stadiums. The introduction of the retractable roof has even made it possible to have grass under domes, so let us all hope that by the turn of the century we will have seen the last of the carpets. This game was not meant to be played on a pool table.

There is, of course, much that baseball should do in the future but probably won't. Some form of profit sharing from local broadcasting revenue has long been indicated as a way of keeping the small-market franchises alive and putting a plug in the owners' incessant poor-mouthing. But no one has yet been able to convince the media-rich fat cats of the urgency of such measures, this despite the obvious example of the NFL. And maybe no one ever will, even if the financial future of the game depends on it.

The office of the baseball commissioner should be restructured in such a way that the occupant ceases to be the figurehead he now is. The commissioner should be elected by and paid by the owners, the players and the umpires. Then, perhaps, the officeholder can be said to represent the game as a whole, not just one part of it. Let the owners have their own chairman of the board or CEO and the players and the umps have their union people. But operating independently there should be a commissioner whose only concern is preserving the integrity and plotting the future of the game.

What also is to become of the dread designated hitter? The 10th man theme has long created discord in the World Series. Do we use this extra player every other year or in every other ballpark? And what is to be done with him now that interleague play has become a reality? The leagues may be anxious to preserve their separate identities, but to play under different rules is ludicrous. Why not return to that old rule that declares there shall be nine men to a side? Maybe by the year 2000 or so, the one-dimensional DH will have gone the way of the green rug.

There seems to be a growing awareness, heightened perhaps by the Marge Schott unpleasantness, that baseball has rested too long on its Jackie Robinson laurels. The game will never truly be integrated until room is made in the front offices for minority executives. It is one thing to be represented on the field, quite another to be excluded from the decision-making process in the boardroom. There should be no question that there are qualified African-

JAPAN: FERTILE FOREIGN SOIL FOR AMERICA'S GAME.

Americans out there who can run a front office. We already know there is one who can run a league and one who can lead a team to victory in the World Series. And the search need not be confined to the playing field. The Oakland Athletics' Sandy Alderson, who had no previous baseball experience, has been one of the most successful general managers of the past decade. Why shouldn't a minority executive outside the game have the same chance to succeed? Why not look for future candidates in law schools or graduate schools of business? Baseball should no longer be a closed fraternity. There may well be fans out there who can run the game better than the professionals. They could hardly do worse.

Finally, there is the future of international competition. As our players' performance in recent Olympic Games has demonstrated, we in this country no longer have a monopoly on baseball talent. We should, in fact, rejoice in the knowledge that our national pastime is fast becoming a world pastime. The Japanese have long had professional leagues, and the experience of Americans who have played in them has

shown that the caliber of play is not significantly below our standards. One need look no further than Los Angeles, where Dodger pitcher Hideo Nomo is dominating the competition, to recognize the vitality of the Japanese game. Baseball is growing rapidly in popularity in Australia as well. The Italians are playing it. And so now are the Russians. It is *the* sport in the Caribbean and much of Central America. Just think of all the marvelous players who have come to the major leagues from Puerto Rico and the Dominican Republic. Cuba, long dominant in amateur baseball, may well have enough stars to staff a major league of its own.

If the game continues to grow worldwide, will it not be both arrogant and absurd to call our World Series winner the "world champion?" It seems inevitable then that, with all of the wondrous new developments in transportation and communication, there should someday be a true World Series. We may be the best at the game now, but who can say what changes time will have wrought? That's the trouble with the future: We can never know it as well as the past. And maybe that's just as well.

Appendix

WORLD SERIES CHAMPIONS

Year	Champion	Score	National League Champion	Record	American League Champion	Record
1905	New York Giants	4–1	New York Giants	105–48	Philadelphia Athletics	92–56
1906	Chicago White Sox	4–2	Chicago Cubs	116–36	Chicago White Sox	93–58
1907	Chicago Cubs	4–0 (1 tie)	Chicago Cubs	107–45	Detroit Tigers	92–58
1908	Chicago Cubs	4–1	Chicago Cubs	99–55	Detroit Tigers	90–63
1909	Pittsburgh Pirates	4–3	Pittsburgh Pirates	110–42	Detroit Tigers	98–54
1910	Philadelphia Athletics	4–1	Chicago Cubs	104–50	Philadelphia Athletics	102–48
1911	Philadelphia Athletics	4–2	New York Giants	99–54	Philadelphia Athletics	101–50
1912	Boston Red Sox	4–3 (1 tie)	New York Giants	103–48	Boston Red Sox	105–47
1913	Philadelphia Athletics	4–1	New York Giants	101–51	Philadelphia Athletics	96–57
1914	Boston Braves	4–0	Boston Braves	94–59	Philadelphia Athletics	99–53
1915	Boston Red Sox	4–1	Philadelphia Phillies	90–62	Boston Red Sox	101–50
1916	Boston Red Sox	4–1	Brooklyn Robins	94–60	Boston Red Sox	91–63
1917	Chicago White Sox	4–2	New York Giants	98–56	Chicago White Sox	100–54
1918	Boston Red Sox	4–2	Chicago Cubs	84–45	Boston Red Sox	75–51
1919	Cincinnati Reds	5–3	Cincinnati Reds	96–44	Chicago White Sox	88–52
1920	Cleveland Indians	5–2	Brooklyn Robins	93–61	Cleveland Indians	98–56
1921	New York Giants	5–3	New York Giants	94–59	New York Yankees	98–55
1922	New York Giants	4–0 (1 tie)	New York Giants	93–61	New York Yankees	94–60
1923	New York Yankees	4–2	New York Giants	95–58	New York Yankees	98–54
1924	Washington Senators	4–3	New York Giants	93–60	Washington Senators	92–62
1925	Pittsburgh Pirates	4–3	Pittsburgh Pirates	95–58	Washington Senators	96–55
1926	St. Louis Cardinals	4–3	St. Louis Cardinals	89–65	New York Yankees	91–63
1927	New York Yankees	4–0	Pittsburgh Pirates	94–60	New York Yankees	110–44
1928	New York Yankees	4–0	St. Louis Cardinals	95–59	New York Yankees	101–53
1929	Philadelphia Athletics	4–1	Chicago Cubs	98–54	Philadelphia Athletics	104–46
1930	Philadelphia Athletics	4–2	St. Louis Cardinals	92–62	Philadelphia Athletics	102–52
1931	St. Louis Cardinals	4–3	St. Louis Cardinals	101–53	Philadelphia Athletics	107–45
1932	New York Yankees	4–0	Chicago Cubs	90–64	New York Yankees	107–47
1933	New York Giants	4–1	New York Giants	91–61	Washington Senators	99–53
1934	St. Louis Cardinals	4–3	St. Louis Cardinals	95–58	Detroit Tigers	101–53
1935	Detroit Tigers	4–2	Chicago Cubs	100–54	Detroit Tigers	93–58
1936	New York Yankees	4–2	New York Giants	92–62	New York Yankees	102–51
1937	New York Yankees	4–1	New York Giants	95–57	New York Yankees	102–52
1938	New York Yankees	4–0	Chicago Cubs	89–63	New York Yankees	99–53
1939	New York Yankees	4–0	Cincinnati Reds	97–57	New York Yankees	106–45
1940	Cincinnati Reds	4–3	Cincinnati Reds	100–53	Detroit Tigers	90–64
1941	New York Yankees	4–1	Brooklyn Dodgers	100–54	New York Yankees	101–53
1942	St. Louis Cardinals	4–1	St. Louis Cardinals	106–48	New York Yankees	103–51
1943	New York Yankees	4–1	St. Louis Cardinals	105–49	New York Yankees	98–56
1944	St. Louis Cardinals	4–2	St. Louis Cardinals	105–49	St. Louis Browns	89–65
1945	Detroit Tigers	4–3	Chicago Cubs	98–56	Detroit Tigers	88–65
1946	St. Louis Cardinals	4–3	St. Louis Cardinals	98–58	Boston Red Sox	104–50
1947	New York Yankees	4–3	Brooklyn Dodgers	94–60	New York Yankees	97–57
1948	Cleveland Indians	4–2	Boston Braves	91–62	Cleveland Indians	97–58
1949	New York Yankees	4–1	Brooklyn Dodgers	97–57	New York Yankees	97–57
1950	New York Yankees	4–0	Philadelphia Phillies	91–63	New York Yankees	98–56
1951	New York Yankees	4–2	New York Giants	98–59	New York Yankees	98–56
1952	New York Yankees	4–3	Brooklyn Dodgers	96–57	New York Yankees	95–59
1953	New York Yankees	4–2	Brooklyn Dodgers	105–49	New York Yankees	99–52
1954	New York Giants	4–0	New York Giants	97–57	Cleveland Indians	111–43

Year	Champion	Score	National League Champion	Record	American League Champion	Record
1955	Brooklyn Dodgers	4–3	Brooklyn Dodgers	98–55	New York Yankees	96–58
1956	New York Yankees	4–3	Brooklyn Dodgers	93–61	New York Yankees	97–57
1957	Milwaukee Braves	4–3	Milwaukee Braves	95–59	New York Yankees	98–56
1958	New York Yankees	4–3	Milwaukee Braves	92–62	New York Yankees	92–62
1959	Los Angeles Dodgers	4–2	Los Angeles Dodgers	88–68	Chicago White Sox	94–60
1960	Pittsburgh Pirates	4–3	Pittsburgh Pirates	95–59	New York Yankees	97–57
1961	New York Yankees	4–1	Cincinnati Reds	93–61	New York Yankees	109–53
1962	New York Yankees	4–3	San Francisco Giants	103–62	New York Yankees	96–66
1963	Los Angeles Dodgers	4–0	Los Angeles Dodgers	99–63	New York Yankees	104–57
1964	St. Louis Cardinals	4–3	St. Louis Cardinals	93–69	New York Yankees	99–63
1965	Los Angeles Dodgers	4–3	Los Angeles Dodgers	97–65	Minnesota Twins	102–60
1966	Baltimore Orioles	4–0	Los Angeles Dodgers	95–67	Baltimore Orioles	97–63
1967	St. Louis Cardinals	4–3	St. Louis Cardinals	101–60	Boston Red Sox	92–70
1968	Detroit Tigers	4–3	St. Louis Cardinals	97–65	Detroit Tigers	103–59
1969	New York Mets	4–1	New York Mets	100–62	Baltimore Orioles	109–53
1970	Baltimore Orioles	4–1	Cincinnati Reds	102–60	Baltimore Orioles	108–54
1971	Pittsburgh Pirates	4–3	Pittsburgh Pirates	97–65	Baltimore Orioles	101–57
1972	Oakland Athletics	4–3	Cincinnati Reds	95–59	Oakland Athletics	93–62
1973	Oakland Athletics	4–3	New York Mets	82–79	Oakland Athletics	94–68
1974	Oakland Athletics	4–1	Los Angeles Dodgers	102–60	Oakland Athletics	90–72
1975	Cincinnati Reds	4–3	Cincinnati Reds	108–54	Boston Red Sox	95–65
1976	Cincinnati Reds	4–0	Cincinnati Reds	102–60	New York Yankees	97–62
1977	New York Yankees	4–2	Los Angeles Dodgers	98–64	New York Yankees	100–62
1978	New York Yankees	4–2	Los Angeles Dodgers	95–67	New York Yankees	100–63
1979	Pittsburgh Pirates	4–3	Pittsburgh Pirates	98–64	Baltimore Orioles	102–57
1980	Philadelphia Phillies	4–2	Philadelphia Phillies	91–71	Kansas City Royals	97–65
1981	Los Angeles Dodgers	4–2	Los Angeles Dodgers	63–47	New York Yankees	59–48
1982	St. Louis Cardinals	4–3	St. Louis Cardinals	92–70	Milwaukee Brewers	95–67
1983	Baltimore Orioles	4–1	Philadelphia Phillies	90–72	Baltimore Orioles	98–64
1984	Detroit Tigers	4–1	San Diego Padres	92–70	Detroit Tigers	104–58
1985	Kansas City Royals	4–3	St. Louis Cardinals	101–61	Kansas City Royals	91–71
1986	New York Mets	4–3	New York Mets	108–54	Boston Red Sox	95–66
1987	Minnesota Twins	4–3	St. Louis Cardinals	95–67	Minnesota Twins	85–77
1988	Los Angeles Dodgers	4–1	Los Angeles Dodgers	94–67	Oakland Athletics	104–58
1989	Oakland Athletics	4–0	San Francisco Giants	92–70	Oakland Athletics	99–63
1990	Cincinnati Reds	4–0	Cincinnati Reds	91–71	Oakland Athletics	103–59
1991	Minnesota Twins	4–3	Atlanta Braves	94–68	Minnesota Twins	95–67
1992	Toronto Blue Jays	4–2	Atlanta Braves	98–64	Toronto Blue Jays	96–66
1993	Toronto Blue Jays	4–2	Philadelphia Phillies	97–65	Toronto Blue Jays	95–67
1994	Series canceled due to strike					
1995	Atlanta Braves	4–2	Atlanta Braves	90–54	Cleveland Indians	100–44
1996	New York Yankees	4–2	Atlanta Braves	96–66	New York Yankees	92–70

MOST VALUABLE PLAYERS

Year	Winner	Team	Position	Key Statistics
1955	Johnny Podres	Brooklyn Dodgers	Pitcher	2–0, 10 strikeouts, 1.00 ERA
1956	Don Larsen	New York Yankees	Pitcher	1–0, perfect game
1957	Lew Burdette	Milwaukee Braves	Pitcher	3–0, 13 strikeouts, 0.67 ERA
1958	Bob Turley	New York Yankees	Pitcher	2–1, 13 strikeouts, 2.76 ERA
1959	Larry Sherry	Los Angeles Dodgers	Pitcher	2–0, 0.71 ERA
1960	Bobby Richardson	New York Yankees	Second Baseman	11 for 30 (.367), 12 RBIs
1961	Whitey Ford	New York Yankees	Pitcher	2–0, 0.00 ERA
1962	Ralph Terry	New York Yankees	Pitcher	2–1, 16 strikeouts, 1.80 ERA
1963	Sandy Koufax	Los Angeles Dodgers	Pitcher	2–0, 23 strikeouts, 1.50

MOST VALUABLE PLAYERS (continued)

Year	Winner	Team	Position	Key Statistics
1964	Bob Gibson	St. Louis Cardinals	Pitcher	2–1, 31 strikeouts, 3.00 ERA
1965	Sandy Koufax	Los Angeles Dodgers	Pitcher	2–1, 29 strikeouts, 0.38 ERA
1966	Frank Robinson	Baltimore Orioles	Outfielder	4 for 14 (.286), 2 HR, 3 RBI
1967	Bob Gibson	St. Louis Cardinals	Pitcher	3–0, 26 strikeouts, 1.00 ERA
1968	Mickey Lolich	Detroit Tigers	Pitcher	3–0, 21 strikeouts, 1.67 ERA
1969	Donn Clendenon	New York Mets	First Baseman	5 for 14 (.357), 3 HR, 4 RBI
1970	Brooks Robinson	Baltimore Orioles	Third Baseman	9 for 21 (.429), 2 HR, 6 RBI
1971	Roberto Clemente	Pittsburgh Pirates	Outfielder	12 for 29 (.414), 2 HR, 4 RBI
1972	Gene Tenace	Oakland Athletics	Catcher	8 for 23 (.348), 4 HR, 9 RBI
1973	Reggie Jackson	Oakland Athletics	Outfielder	9 for 29 (.310), 1 HR, 6 RBI
1974	Rollie Fingers	Oakland Athletics	Relief Pitcher	1–0, 2 saves, 1.93 ERA
1975	Pete Rose	Cincinnati Reds	Third Baseman	10 for 27 (.370), 3 runs scored
1976	Johnny Bench	Cincinnati Reds	Catcher	8 for 15 (.533), 2 HR, 6 RBI
1977	Reggie Jackson	New York Yankees	DH	9 for 20 (.450), 5 HR, 8 RBI
1978	Bucky Dent	New York Yankees	Shortstop	10 for 24 (.417), 3 runs, 7 RBI
1979	Willie Stargell	Pittsburgh Pirates	First Baseman	12 for 30 (.400), 3 HR, 7 RBI
1980	Mike Schmidt	Philadelphia Phillies	Third Baseman	8 for 21 (.381), 2 HR, 7 RBI
1981	Ron Cey	Los Angeles Dodgers	Third Baseman	7 for 20 (.350), 1 HR, 6 RBI
	Pedro Guerrero	Los Angeles Dodgers	Outfielder	7 for 21 (.333), 2 HR, 7 RBI
	Steve Yeager	Los Angeles Dodgers	Catcher	4 for 14 (.286), 2 HR, 4 RBI
1982	Darrell Porter	St. Louis Cardinals	Catcher	8 for 28 (.286), 1 HR, 5 RBI
1983	Rick Dempsey	Baltimore Orioles	Catcher	5 for 13 (.385), 1 HR, 2 RBI
1984	Alan Trammell	Detroit Tigers	Shortstop	9 for 20 (.450), 2 HR, 6 RBI
1985	Bret Saberhagen	Kansas City Royals	Pitcher	2–0, 10 strikeouts, 0.50
1986	Ray Knight	New York Mets	Third Baseman	9 for 23 (.391), 1 HR, 5 RBI
1987	Frank Viola	Minnesota Twins	Pitcher	2–1, 16 strikeouts, 3.72 ERA
1988	Orel Hershiser	Los Angeles Dodgers	Pitcher	2–0, 17 strikeouts, 1.00 ERA
1989	Dave Stewart	Oakland Athletics	Pitcher	2–0, 14 strikeouts, 1.69 ERA
1990	Jose Rijo	Cincinnati Reds	Pitcher	2–0, 14 strikeouts, 0.59 ERA
1991	Jack Morris	Minnesota Twins	Pitcher	2–0, 15 strikeouts, 1.17 ERA
1992	Pat Borders	Toronto Blue Jays	Catcher	9 for 20 (.450), 1 HR, 3 RBI
1993	Paul Molitor	Toronto Blue Jays	DH	12 for 24 (.500), 2 HR, 8 RBI
1994	Series canceled due to strike			
1995	Tom Glavine	Atlanta Braves	Pitcher	2–0, 11 strikeouts, 1.29 ERA
1996	John Wetteland	New York Yankees	Pitcher	4 saves, 4 strikeouts, 2.08 ERA

CAREER RECORDS

BATTING

GAMES

Yogi Berra	75
Mickey Mantle	65
Elston Howard	54
Hank Bauer	53
Gil McDougald	53
Phil Rizzuto	52
Joe DiMaggio	51
Frankie Frisch	50
Pee Wee Reese	44
Roger Maris	41
Babe Ruth	41
Carl Furillo	40
Bill Skowron	39
Gil Hodges	39
Jim Gilliam	39
Bill Dickey	38
Jackie Robinson	38
Tony Kubek	37
Three tied with	36

AT BATS

Yogi Berra	259
Mickey Mantle	230
Joe DiMaggio	199
Frankie Frisch	197
Gil McDougald	190
Hank Bauer	188

CAREER RECORDS (continued)

BATTING (cont'd)

AT BATS (cont'd)
Phil Rizzuto	183
Elston Howard	171
Pee Wee Reese	169
Roger Maris	152
Jim Gilliam	147
Tony Kubek	146
Bill Dickey	145
Jackie Robinson	137
Bill Skowron	133
Duke Snider	133
Gil Hodges	131
Bobby Richardson	131
Pete Rose	130
Babe Ruth	129
Bob Meusel	129
Goose Goslin	129

HITS
Yogi Berra	71
Mickey Mantle	59
Frankie Frisch	58
Joe DiMaggio	54
Pee Wee Reese	46
Hank Bauer	46
Phil Rizzuto	45
Gil McDougald	45
Lou Gehrig	43
Eddie Collins	42
Babe Ruth	42
Elston Howard	42
Bobby Richardson	40
Bill Skowron	39
Duke Snider	38
Bill Dickey	37
Goose Goslin	37
Steve Garvey	36
Gil Hodges	35
Tony Kubek	35
Pete Rose	35
Reggie Jackson	35

BATTING AVERAGE (Minimum 50 at bats)
Pepper Martin	.418
Paul Molitor	.418
Marquis Grissom	.404
Lou Brock	.391
Thurman Munson	.373
George Brett	.373
Hank Aaron	.364
Frank Baker	.363
Roberto Clemente	.362

Lou Gehrig	.361
Reggie Jackson	.357
Carl Yastrzemski	.352
Earle Combs	.350
Stan Hack	.348
Joe Jackson	.345
Jimmie Foxx	.344
Julian Javier	.333
Billy Martin	.333
Al Simmons	.329
Eddie Collins	.328

HOME RUNS
Mickey Mantle	18
Babe Ruth	15
Yogi Berra	12
Duke Snider	11
Reggie Jackson	10
Lou Gehrig	10
Frank Robinson	8
Bill Skowron	8
Joe DiMaggio	8
Goose Goslin	7
Hank Bauer	7
Gil McDougald	7
Roger Maris	6
Al Simmons	6
Reggie Smith	6
Bill Dickey	6
Hank Greenberg	5
Gil Hodges	5
Elston Howard	5
Charlie Keller	5
Billy Martin	5
Johnny Bench	5

RUNS BATTED IN
Mickey Mantle	40
Yogi Berra	39
Lou Gehrig	35
Babe Ruth	33
Joe DiMaggio	30
Bill Skowron	29
Duke Snider	26
Reggie Jackson	24
Bill Dickey	24
Hank Bauer	24
Gil McDougald	24
Hank Greenberg	22
Gil Hodges	21
Goose Goslin	19
Elston Howard	19
Tony Lazzeri	19

CAREER RECORDS (continued)

BATTING (cont'd)

RUNS BATTED IN (cont'd)
Billy Martin 19
Roger Maris 18
Frank Baker 18
Charlie Keller 18

RUNS
Mickey Mantle 42
Yogi Berra 41
Babe Ruth 37
Lou Gehrig 30
Joe DiMaggio 27
Roger Maris 26
Elston Howard 25
Gil McDougald 23
Jackie Robinson 22
Gene Woodling 21
Reggie Jackson 21
Duke Snider 21
Phil Rizzuto 21
Hank Bauer 21
Pee Wee Reese 20
Eddie Collins 20
Bill Dickey 19
Bill Skowron 19
Frank Robinson 19

STOLEN BASES
Lou Brock 14
Eddie Collins 14
Frank Chance 10
Davey Lopes 10
Phil Rizzuto 10
Honus Wagner 9
Frankie Frisch 9
Johnny Evers 8
Pepper Martin 7
Joe Morgan 7
Joe Tinker 6
Vince Coleman 6
Jackie Robinson 6
Jimmy Slagle 6
Maury Wills 6
Bobby Tolan 6
Rickey Henderson 6

TOTAL BASES
Mickey Mantle 123
Yogi Berra 117
Babe Ruth 96
Lou Gehrig 87
Joe DiMaggio 84

Duke Snider 79
Hank Bauer 75
Reggie Jackson 74
Frankie Frisch 74
Gil McDougald 72
Bill Skowron 69
Elston Howard 66
Goose Goslin 63
Pee Wee Reese 59
Lou Brock 57
Roger Maris 56
Billy Martin 56
Bill Dickey 55
Gil Hodges 54
Phil Rizzuto 54

SLUGGING AVERAGE (Minimum 50 at bats)
Reggie Jackson 755
Babe Ruth 744
Lou Gehrig 731
Al Simmons 658
Lou Brock 655
Paul Molitor 636
Pepper Martin 636
Hank Greenberg 624
Charlie Keller 611
Jimmie Foxx 609
Dave Henderson 606
Hank Aaron 600
Duke Snider 594
Billy Martin 566
Carl Yastrzemski 556
Frank Robinson 554
Frank Baker 538
Mickey Mantle 535
Roberto Clemente 534
Gene Tenace 529
Gene Woodling 529

STRIKEOUTS
Mickey Mantle 54
Elston Howard 37
Duke Snider 33
Babe Ruth 30
Gil McDougald 29
Bill Skowron 26
Hank Bauer 25
Reggie Jackson 24
Bob Meusel 24
Frank Robinson 23
George Kelly 23
Tony Kubek 23
Joe DiMaggio 23
Joe Collins 22

CAREER RECORDS (continued)

BATTING (cont'd)

STRIKEOUTS (cont'd)
Jim Bottomley 22
Roger Maris 21
Steve Garvey 21
Tony Perez 21
Three tied with 20

PITCHING

GAMES
Whitey Ford 22
Rollie Fingers 16
Allie Reynolds 15
Bob Turley 15
Clay Carroll 14
Clem Labine 13
Waite Hoyt 12
Catfish Hunter 12
Art Nehf 12
Paul Derringer 11
Carl Erskine 11
Rube Marquard 11
Christy Mathewson 11
Vic Raschi 11
Chief Bender 10
Don Larsen 10
Herb Pennock 10
Red Ruffing 10
Pedro Borbon 10
Don Gullett 10

INNINGS PITCHED
Whitey Ford 146
Christy Mathewson 101⅔
Red Ruffing 85⅔
Chief Bender 85
Waite Hoyt 83⅔
Bob Gibson 81
Art Nehf 79
Allie Reynolds 77⅓
Jim Palmer 65
Catfish Hunter 63
George Earnshaw 62⅔
Joe Bush 60⅔
Vic Raschi 60⅓
Rube Marquard 58⅔
George Mullin 58
Three Finger Brown 57⅔
Carl Mays 57⅓
Sandy Koufax 57
Burleigh Grimes 56⅔
Warren Spahn 55

WINS
Whitey Ford 10
Bob Gibson 7
Red Ruffing 7
Allie Reynolds 7
Lefty Gomez 6
Chief Bender 6
Waite Hoyt 6
Jack Coombs 5
Three Finger Brown 5
Herb Pennock 5
Christy Mathewson 5
Vic Raschi 5
Catfish Hunter 5

LOSSES
Whitey Ford 8
Eddie Plank 5
Schoolboy Rowe 5
Joe Bush 5
Rube Marquard 5
Christy Mathewson 5
Chief Bender 4
Three Finger Brown 4
Paul Derringer 4
Bill Donovan 4
Burleigh Grimes 4
Waite Hoyt 4
Carl Mays 4
Art Nehf 4
Don Newcombe 4
Bill Sherdel 4
Ed Summers 4
Ralph Terry 4

SAVES
Rollie Fingers 6
Allie Reynolds 4
John Wetteland 4
Johnny Murphy 4
Roy Face 3
Herb Pennock 3
Kent Tekulve 3
Firpo Marberry 3
Will McEnaney 3
Todd Worrell 3
Tug McGraw 3

EARNED RUN AVERAGE (Minimum 25 innings pitched)
Jack Billingham 0.36
Harry Brecheen 0.83
Babe Ruth 0.87

PITCHING (cont'd)

EARNED RUN AVERAGE (continued)

Sherry Smith	0.89
Sandy Koufax	0.95
Hippo Vaughn	1.00
Monte Pearson	1.01
Christy Mathewson	1.15
Babe Adams	1.29
Eddie Plank	1.32
Rollie Fingers	1.35
Wild Bill Hallahan	1.36
George Earnshaw	1.58
Spud Chandler	1.62
Mickey Lolich	1.67
Jesse Haines	1.67
Max Lanier	1.71
Jesse Barnes	1.71
Stan Covaleski	1.74
Lefty Grove	1.75
Orval Overall	1.75

SHUTOUTS

Christy Mathewson	4
Three Finger Brown	3
Whitey Ford	3
Wild Bill Hallahan	2
Lew Burdette	2
Bill Dinneen	2
Sandy Koufax	2
Allie Reynolds	2
Art Nehf	2
Bob Gibson	2

COMPLETE GAMES

Christy Mathewson	10
Chief Bender	9
Bob Gibson	8
Red Ruffing	7
Whitey Ford	7
George Mullin	6
Eddie Plank	6
Art Nehf	6
Waite Hoyt	6
Three Finger Brown	5
Joe Bush	5
Bill Donovan	5

George Earnshaw	5
Walter Johnson	5
Carl Mays	5
Deacon Phillips	5
Allie Reynolds	5

STRIKEOUTS

Whitey Ford	94
Bob Gibson	92
Allie Reynolds	62
Sandy Koufax	61
Red Ruffing	61
Chief Bender	59
George Earnshaw	56
Waite Hoyt	49
Christy Mathewson	48
Bob Turley	46
Jim Palmer	44
Vic Raschi	43
Jack Morris	40
Don Gullett	37
Don Drysdale	36
Lefty Grove	36

BASES ON BALLS

Whitey Ford	34
Allie Reynolds	32
Art Nehf	32
Jim Palmer	31
Bob Turley	29
Paul Derringer	27
Red Ruffing	27
Don Gullett	26
Burleigh Grimes	26
Vic Raschi	25
Carl Erskine	24
Wild Bill Hallahan	23
Waite Hoyt	22
Chief Bender	21
Jack Coombs	21
Joe Bush	20
Tom Glavine	20
Don Larsen	19
Dave McNally	19
Hal Schumacher	19

SINGLE SERIES RECORDS

BATTING

RUNS

Player, Team	Year	Series Length	No.
Reggie Jackson, New York Yankees	1977	6	10
Paul Molitor, Toronto Blue Jays	1993	6	10
Babe Ruth, New York Yankees	1928	4	9
Lou Gehrig, New York Yankees	1932	4	9
Roy White, New York Yankees	1978	6	9
Lenny Dykstra, Philadelphia Phillies	1993	6	9
Earle Combs, New York Yankees	1932	4	8
Charlie Keller, New York Yankees	1927	4	8
Babe Ruth, New York Yankees	1923	6	8
Jack Powell, New York Yankees	1936	6	8
Tommy Leach, Pittsburgh Pirates	1909	7	8
Pepper Martin, St. Louis Cardinals	1934	7	8
Billy Johnson, New York Yankees	1947	7	8
Mickey Mantle, New York Yankees	1960	7	8
Bobby Richardson, New York Yankees	1960	7	8
Mickey Mantle, New York Yankees	1964	7	8
Lou Brock, St. Louis Cardinals	1967	7	8

HITS

Player, Team	Year	Series Length	No.
Bobby Richardson, New York Yankees	1960	7	13
Lou Brock, St. Louis Cardinals	1968	7	13
Marty Barrett, Boston Red Sox	1986	7	13
Billy Martin, New York Yankees	1953	6	12
Sam Rice, Washington Senators	1925	7	12
Pepper Martin, St. Louis Cardinals	1931	7	12
Bill Skowron, New York Yankees	1960	7	12
Lou Brock, St. Louis Cardinals	1967	7	12
Roberto Clemente, Pittsburgh Pirates	1971	7	12
Willie Stargell, Pittsburgh Pirates	1979	7	12
Phil Garner, Pittsburgh Pirates	1979	7	12
Robin Yount, Milwaukee Brewers	1982	7	12
Buck Herzog, New York Giants	1912	8	12
Joe Jackson, Chicago White Sox	1919	8	12
Marquis Grissom, Atlanta Braves	1996	6	12
Paul Molitor, Toronto Blue Jays	1993	6	12
Roberto Alomar, Toronto Blue Jays	1993	6	12

STOLEN BASES

Player, Team	Year	Series Length	No.
Lou Brock, St. Louis Cardinals	1967	7	7
Lou Brock, St. Louis Cardinals	1968	7	7
Jimmy Slagle, Chicago Cubs	1907	5	6
Honus Wagner, Pittsburgh Pirates	1909	7	6
Vince Coleman, St. Louis Cardinals	1986	7	6
Ken Lofton, Cleveland Indians	1995	6	6
Frank Chance, Chicago Cubs	1908	5	5
Pepper Martin, St. Louis Cardinals	1931	7	5
Bobby Tolan, Cincinnati Reds	1972	7	5
Otis Nixon, Atlanta Braves	1992	6	5
Deion Sanders, Atlanta Braves	1992	6	5

HOME RUNS

Player, Team	Year	Series Length	No.
Reggie Jackson, New York Yankees	1977	6	5
Lou Gehrig, New York Yankees	1928	4	4
Willie Aikens, Kansas City Royals	1980	6	4
Babe Ruth, New York Yankees	1928	7	4
Duke Snider, Brooklyn Dodgers	1952	7	4
Duke Snider, Brooklyn Dodgers	1955	7	4
Hank Bauer, New York Yankees	1958	7	4
Gene Tenace, Oakland Athletics	1972	7	4
Lenny Dykstra, Philadelphia Phillies	1993	6	4

RUNS BATTED IN

Player, Team	Year	Series Length	No.
Bobby Richardson, New York Yankees	1960	7	12
Mickey Mantle, New York Yankees	1960	7	11
Ted Kluszewski, Chicago White Sox	1959	6	10
Yogi Berra, New York Yankees	1956	7	10
Lou Gehrig, New York Yankees	1928	4	9
Danny Murphy, Philadelphia Athletics	1910	5	9
Gene Tenace, Oakland Athletics	1972	7	9
Gary Carter, New York Mets	1986	7	9
Dwight Evans, Boston Red Sox	1986	7	9
Tony Fernandez, Toronto Blue Jays	1993	6	9

BATTING AVERAGE (Minimum 10 At Bats)

Player, Team	Year	Series Length	Avg.
Billy Hatcher, Cincinnati Reds	1990	4	.750
Babe Ruth, New York Yankees	1928	4	.625
Chris Sabo, Cincinati Reds	1990	4	.563
Hank Gowdy, Boston Braves	1914	4	.545
Lou Gehrig, New York Yankees	1928	4	.545
Deion Sanders, Atlanta Braves	1992	6	.533
Johnny Bench, Cincinnati Reds	1976	4	.533
Dane Iorg, St. Louis Cardinals	1982	7	.529
Lou Gehrig, New York Yankees	1932	4	.529
Thurman Munson, New York Yankees	1976	4	.529

SLUGGING AVERAGE (Minimum 10 At Bats)

Player, Team	Year	Series Length	Avg.
Charlie Keller, New York Yankees	1939	4	1.818
Lou Gehrig, New York Yankees	1928	4	1.727
Babe Ruth, New York Yankees	1928	4	1.375
Hank Gowdy, Boston Braves	1914	4	1.273
Reggie Jackson, New York Yankees	1977	6	1.250
Billy Hatcher, Cincinnati Reds	1990	4	1.250
Johnny Bench, Cincinnati Reds	1976	4	1.133
Lou Gehrig, New York Yankees	1932	4	1.118
Willie Aikens, Kansas City Royals	1980	6	1.110
Johnny Mize, New York Yankees	1952	7	1.106
Johnny Blanchard, New York Yankees	1961	5	1.100

SINGLE SERIES RECORDS (continued)

PITCHING

COMPLETE GAMES

Player, Team	Year	Series Length	No.
Christy Mathewson, New York Giants	1905	5	3
Jack Coombs, Philadelphia Athletics	1910	5	3
Chief Bender, Philadelphia Athletics	1911	6	3
Hippo Vaughn, Chicago Cubs	1918	6	3
Babe Adams, Pittsburgh Pirates	1909	7	3
George Mullin, Detroit Tigers	1909	7	3
Stan Covaleski, Cleveland Indians	1920	7	3
Walter Johnson, Washington Senators	1925	7	3
Bobo Newsom, Detroit Tigers	1940	7	3
Lew Burdette, Milwaukee Brewers	1957	7	3
Bob Gibson, St. Louis Cardinals	1967	7	3
Bob Gibson, St;. Louis Cardinals	1968	7	3
Mickey Lolich, Detroit Tigers	1968	7	3

SHUTOUTS

Player, Team	Year	Series Length	No.
Christy Mathewson, New York Giants	1905	5	3
Lew Burdette, Milwaukee Brewers	1957	7	2
Whitey Ford, New York Yankees	1960	7	2
Sandy Koufax, Los Angeles Dodgers	1965	7	2

INNINGS PITCHED

Player, Team	Year	Series Length	No.
George Mullin, Detroit Tigers	1909	7	32
Warren Spahn, Milwaukee Brewers	1958	7	28⅔
Christy Mathewson, New York Giants	1912	8	28⅔
Christy Mathewson, New York Giants	1905	5	27
Jack Coombs, Philadelphia Athletics	1910	5	27
Christy Mathewson, New York Giants	1911	6	27
Red Faber, Chicago White Sox	1917	6	27
Hippo Vaughn, Chicago Cubs	1918	6	27
Babe Adams, Pittsburgh Pirates	1909	7	27
Stan Covaleski, Cleveland Indians	1920	7	27
Lew Burdette, Milwaukee Brewers	1957	7	27
Bob Gibson, St. Louis Cardinals	1964	7	27
Bob Gibson, St. Louis Cardinals	1967	7	27
Bob Gibson, St. Louis Cardinals	1968	7	27
Mickey Lolich, Detroit Tigers	1968	7	27
Waite Hoyt, New York Yankees	1921	8	27

STRIKEOUTS

Player, Team	Year	Series Length	No.
Bob Gibson, St. Louis Cardinals	1968	7	35
Bob Gibson, St. Louis Cardinals	1964	7	31
Sandy Koufax, Los Angeles Dodgers	1965	7	29
Bob Gibson, St. Louis Cardinals	1967	7	26
Sandy Koufax, Los Angeles Dodgers	1963	4	23
Hal Newhouser, Detroit Tigers	1945	7	22
Mickey Lolich, Detroit Tigers	1968	7	21
Smokey Joe Wood, Boston Red Sox	1912	8	21
Chief Bender, Philadelphia Athletics	1911	6	20
George Mullin, Detroit Tigers	1909	7	20
Walter Johnson, Washington Senators	1924	7	20
George Earnshaw, Philadelphia A's	1931	7	20

WINS

Player, Team	Year	Series Length	No.
Christy Mathewson, New York Giants	1905	5	3
Jack Coombs, Philadelphia Athletics	1910	5	3
Red Faber, Chicago White Sox	1917	6	3
Babe Adams, Pittsburgh Pirates	1909	7	3
Stan Covaleski, Cleveland Indians	1920	7	3
Harry Brecheen, St. Louis Cardinals	1946	7	3
Lew Burdette, Milwaukee Braves	1957	7	3
Bob Gibson, St. Louis Cardinals	1967	7	3
Mickey Lolich, Detroit Tigers	1968	7	3
Smokey Joe Wood, Boston Red Sox	1912	8	3

SAVES

Player, Team	Year	Series Length	No.
John Wetteland, New York Yankees	1996	6	4
Roy Face, Pittsburgh Pirates	1960	7	3
Kent Tekulve, Pittsburgh Pirates	1979	7	3

EARNED RUN AVERAGE (Minimum 14 innings)

Player, Team	Year	Innings Pitched	No.
Christy Mathewson, New York Giants	1905	27	0.00
Waite Hoyt, New York Yankees	1921	27	0.00
Carl Hubbell, New York Giants	1933	20	0.00
Whitey Ford, New York Yankees	1960	18	0.00
Joe McGinnity, New York Giants	1905	17	0.00
Duster Mails, Cleveland Indians	1920	15⅓	0.00
Rube Benton, New York Giants	1917	14	0.00
Whitey Ford, New York Yankees	1961	14	0.00

BIBLIOGRAPHY

Alexander, Charles. *Our Game*. New York: Henry Holt & Company, 1991.

Asinof, Eliot. *Eight Men Out*. New York: Holt, Rinehart and Winston, 1963.

Clark, Tom. *Champagne and Baloney*. New York: Harper and Row, 1976.

Creamer, Robert. *Babe—The Legend Comes to Life*. New York: Simon and Schuster, 1974.

Creamer, Robert. *Stengel—His Life and Times*. New York: Simon and Schuster, 1984.

Durso, Joseph. *The Days of Mr. McGraw*. Englewood Cliffs, New Jersey: Prentice-Hall, Inc., 1969.

Frommer, Harvey. *Shoeless Joe and Ragtime Baseball*. Dallas: Taylor Publishing Company, 1992.

Gallagher, Mark. *Fifty Years of Yankee All Stars*. New York: Leisure Press, 1984.

Golenbock, Peter. *Fenway—An Unexpurgated History of the Boston Red Sox*. New York: G.P. Putnam's Sons, 1992.

Halberstam, David. *Summer of '49*. New York: William Morrow and Company, Inc., 1989.

Henrich, Tommy (with Bill Gilbert). *Five O'Clock Lightning*. New York: Birch Lane Press, 1992.

Kubek Tony and Pluto, Jerry. *Sixty-One*. New York: Fireside, 1987.

Lansche, Jerry. *Glory Fades Away*. Dallas: Taylor Publishing Company, 1991.

Lowry, Philip J. *Green Cathedrals*. Reading, Mass.: Addison-Wesley Publishing Co., Inc., 1992.

Rains, Rob. *The St. Louis Cardinals*. New York: St. Martin's Press, 1992.

Reston, James Jr. *Collision at Home Plate*. New York: Edward Burlingame Books, 1971.

Ritter, Lawrence S. *The Glory of Their Times*. New York: The Macmillan Company, 1966.

Ritter, Lawrence S. *Lost Ballparks*. New York: Viking, 1992.

Sowell, Mike. *The Pitch that Killed*. New York: The Macmillan Company, 1989.

Sowell, Mike. *July 2, 1903*. New York: The Macmillan Company, 1992.

Staten, Vince. *'Ol Diz*. New York: Harper Collins, 1992.

Thorn, John and Palmer, Peter. *Total Baseball*. New York: Warner Books, 1991.

Photography Credits

Index